PRAISE FOR *DIGITAL LIFE*

"The digital transformation of the financial services industry is one of the most significant trends in its history. In this book, Mark and Guillermo provide a unique road map which not only sets out the impacts of digitalization on our lives and on financial services but, importantly, describes the strategic imperatives that will enable credit unions to serve and thrive."

—Jim Nussle, CUDE (He, His) President and CEO, CUNA
Credit Union National Association

"*Digital Life* is not only timely, it also perfectly sets the acceleration of what we thought was the future to NOW! Mark and Guillermo have perfectly partnered to set the playbook for both business and consumers. Fast-follower is no longer good enough, and they appropriately set the bar at the cutting edge as we enter this new era. *Digital Life* is a must-read and a reference guide that you will refer back to often!"

—Chuck Fagan, President and CEO, PSCU

"The agenda proposed in *Digital Life* makes you reflect on the latest trends, where we are going, and how to prepare for it. Digital transformation—because of the impacts of COVID-19—has accelerated in one year what [before] would have taken a decade in the world of IT."

—Hugo Santana Londoño, Regional Consultancy and Delivery Partner General Manager, Microsoft

"In 2020, the world shifted. Disruption went from growing disruption with a small d to extreme Disruption with a capital D. This is a Disruption that knows no boundaries. It also has enriching opportunities for consumers and empowering relationship opportunities for credit unions and other financial institutions. This is a journey that Mark Sievewright has guided us on for some time. In *Digital Life*, Mark and Guillermo provide us with a framework to understand this Disruption and to maximize opportunities both for our members and for our credit unions."

—Brian Branch, President and CEO, World Council of Credit Unions

Digital Life

by Guillermo Kopp and Mark Sievewright

ISBN 978-1-64663-225-1

Published by

◣ köehlerbooks™

3705 Shore Drive
Virginia Beach, VA 23455
800-435-4811
www.koehlerbooks.com

DIGITAL LIFE

MARK SIEVEWRIGHT &
GUILLERMO KOPP

VIRGINIA BEACH
CAPE CHARLES

TABLE OF CONTENTS

1.
VISION STATEMENT

EVER SINCE OUR DAYS WORKING together in the early 2000s at the research and advisory firm, TowerGroup, we have been focused on predicting technology's impact on financial services. As our careers took different paths, that fascination with technology grew into a strong desire to understand the drivers of financial services transformation and to help leadership teams at financial institutions determine what they should be doing about it. This book is the culmination of much of our thinking.

Within today's financial services business, rapidly accelerating technological advances are creating entirely new business models that redefine every aspect of how people and businesses manage their financial lives. New technologies give rise to a massive increase in the availability and use of digital insights, shaping consumer expectations and the ability of financial institutions to use consumer data to price, target, and market their products and services, as well as reshape digital interactions.

To compete and remain relevant, financial firms are adopting new technologies at an ever-increasing pace. Demand for online access, digital collaboration, and immediate response is causing a shift toward more direct and immediate interactions. Digital approaches allow consumers to take more control over their financial lives. Financial firms must shift their focus to demonstrate how they add value, including the provision of exceptional (and personalized) service experiences.

In trying to "find the future", we have defined nine primary areas of transformation. Each of these is described at a high level in this first chapter, followed by deep dives into each throughout the remainder of the book. This shared vision reflects our strong belief that one of the primary roles of leaders is to find and secure the future for their organizations. It is our hope that this book will help you to do so.

In essence the leadership themes underpinning this future vision are as follows:

DIGITAL VALUE

Many financial services executives are wondering whether their physical branches will cease to exist in a decade or so. The real question is about the value that their visitors (whether consumers, clients, customers, members, or the public) will find within those branches. Besides, the globally devastating COVID-19 pandemic has created a lasting reconceptualization of empathic physical proximity, particularly in closed spaces. People began to do everything remotely. Riding on advanced digital technologies, financial institutions will need to reframe the role and operational model of their offices and branches.

In the digital world of the future, consumer value will hinge primarily on the combined digital and physical (in-person) experience. The continuing growth of mobile channels and the adoption of remote working habits will heighten the value of face-to-face interactions through videoconferencing.

The perceived value that individuals will attach to an increasingly commoditized array of financial transactions, credit facilities, investments, and account services will become marginal. To the contrary, the richer lifestyle purpose, localization, sophistication, and timeliness of digital interactions will create new dimensions of value. Such digital experiential value will surpass, possibly by about two orders of magnitude, what people get from traditional physical branches.

Why would digital interactions be worth so much? For starters, digital transactions are practically instantaneous. They are also multidimensional and may encompass various financial and lifestyle services. Most importantly, social media and digital channels may go viral and significantly amplify the experiential impact (hopefully positive) on any one individual. Hence, the immediate collective (or massive) digital momentum may spike and multiply the aggregate value.

GENERATIONAL CHANGES: OKAY, BOOMER!

Demographic change is here! That is *not* news. It is what you've heard *ad nauseam* at countless financial services conferences for the past five years. Demographic change has taken change center stage as the economic, social, and political impact of more people living longer starts to emerge. What *is* news, however, is that the speed of demographic change and development - and the breadth of consequences - will lead to a dramatic shift in the use and consumption of financial services over the next decade.

As you think about this, it would be a really poor generalization to assume all millennials are tech-savvy and boomers have little interest in technology. Remembering that Steve Jobs was fifty-two when he announced the iPhone innovation in 2007, it is hard to understand why many still consider boomers—who dominate the market in terms of money spent on technology—to lack the patience or desire to champion new technology.

However, more mature generational cohorts can learn much from how the younger generations use and adopt technology, particularly at work. Younger generations tend to use technology across all facets of their lives and, as such, have developed effective and efficient methods of understanding, embracing, and interacting with fresh technology innovations.

Figure 1 – Digital life

INTELLIGENT EXPERIENCES

Today, people have little patience for companies that do not meet their sky-high expectations. They demand a superior service experience and, if there is an issue, they want it to be solved immediately and with minimal effort. In this digital age, first impressions are more critical than ever. Financial firms are not immune from these new ground rules and can lose customers or members rapidly—and for good—if the services they offer lack purpose and intuitive access.

The most relevant emerging technologies in financial services center around the notion of delivering intelligent experiences (or interactions) to their clients, customers, or members. "Intelligent" implies the ability to learn from existing interactions to optimize future ones—a simple concept, right? While financial firms will inevitably pursue different paths to create intelligent experiences, data and digital interactions will be the cornerstone they use.

The availability of accurate, up-to-date and high-quality consumer data integrated with insights on their lifestyles and specific needs will determine tomorrow's financial services winners from the losers. The greater the knowledge and understanding of their clients, customers, or members, the easier it will be for financial firms to deliver outstanding, intelligence-based experiences delivering uber-personalization, efficiency, and simplicity. For example, ubiquitous data and digital experiences will drastically transform the role of traditional branches.

NEW ANALYTICS

How will artificial intelligence (AI) technologies change today's dashboards and statistical trends analysis? How will AI transform core financial services processes such as client, customer, and member services, or even risk management? Will AI replace human expertise and wisdom?

In a decade or two, relentless advances in AI such as bots, cognitive services, and machine-learning algorithms, will redefine the broad realm of in-person, call center, and online interactions. By augmenting human intelligence and absorbing menial tasks, advanced AI will enable financial institutions to steer both opportunity and risk situations into mostly desirable outcomes.

Furthermore, new breeds of AI will feature deep and holistic perceptual capabilities (e.g., image recognition and language understanding). Deep-learning algorithms and cognitive services will help financial institutions navigate myriad digital and physical events that take place in an increasingly frantic and interconnected digital world. A big benefit will be the ability to predict future stakeholder and market behaviors with utmost accuracy.

Getting there, however, will require most institutions to break out from conventional analysis and adopt pristine AI methods. Proper use of AI calls for new rules too, such as ensuring that intelligent credit decisions are fully explainable and free from bias.

NATURE OF COMPETITION

The financial services industry is at a tipping point—either disrupt or be disrupted! As start-ups and financial technology (fintech) firms entice digital-minded customers that demand customized and targeted experiences, traditional players must re-think how they do business. Simply put, there are now more options available to both individuals and businesses other than those provided by banks and credit unions.

The value of fintechs to their customers can be measured in the real, everyday difference they make for businesses and individuals. Many have embraced fintechs, and the result so far has been easier online offerings and more competition. Within this, the role of technology has evolved from being a vital enabler in the operating models of the traditional financial firms to driving, shaping, and redefining business models and revenue streams in this new era of Digital Life.

Broad-based access to the latest technological capabilities, coupled with the breakneck speed of change, has destroyed industry barriers to entry. Technology allows born digital start-ups to compete in a highly effective way. To remain relevant, incumbents will need to embrace new organizational models that are simple, agile, and collaborative. Financial firms can deliver exceptional experiences for their clients, customers, or members by partnering with a rich ecosystem of digital providers.

UBER PERSONALIZATION

Pervasive digital interactions will transcend the financial domain and touch virtually every aspect of modern life. A digital mesh of intertwined lifestyle, payments, credit, insurance, and investment services will instantly define most individual needs and wants. Such atomized, multifaceted, and vertiginous digital realities will act upon much finer decision points to attend and delight all sorts of individual preferences. To capitalize on these tiny moments of digital truth, financial institutions will need to sense, understand, and take proactive action within fractions of a second.

What granular information will feed a profound understanding of every individual? First, financial institutions must reach well beyond the much valuable client, customer, and member accounting transactions, financial records, and product preferences that they maintain within their core systems. A holistic view will capture subtle patterns from digital interactions such as individual mood, behavioral traits, social media environment, and situational context.

To obtain such a comprehensive view, financial institutions will need to partner with adjacent industries, such as commerce, manufacturing and services companies, fintechs, and government entities that are leading in digital interactions. Last, they will have to garner a disparate array of financial and non-financial data to tailor their products and services instantly on the spot.

DIGITAL PAYMENTS

Electronic payments are accelerating the transfer of physical and digital goods or services. With the growing prevalence of instant mobile payments and interaction habits, consumers demand ubiquitous access anytime and all the time. Regulators, in the US and around the world, are also stepping in to spark innovation and open the payments domain to a broad ecosystem of digital service providers such as fintechs and companies outside the financial sector.

Rising business and consumer needs for real-time payments within this emerging, fast-paced digital world will compel financial institutions to rearchitect their processes and technologies. Major modernization efforts will include core systems, customer databases, electronic channels, risk management, and compliance platforms. Financial institutions must acknowledge that digital payments will go well beyond the traditional parameters of a financial transaction. Indeed, payments transactions must also capture and convey multifaceted data from the individual and business context.

The accumulation of rich data surrounding a payments transaction will also bring additional value in terms of consumer and market intelligence. For instance, external data captured live in a retailer outlet, can combine with financial insights, and feed advanced machine-learning algorithms. This predictive accuracy will delight consumers and grow the business for all participants in the digital value chain.

DIGITAL VALUE-ADDED SERVICES

As digital technologies weigh in all consumer and business interactions, people will appreciate, and indeed demand, the provision of creative and customized digital services. Understanding digital trends as well as stated and still unarticulated needs, will allow financial institutions to devise successful digital services strategies. Effective service offerings will thrive on availability, convenience, localization, personalization, transparency, and trust.

As innovation in channels, devices, and digital services disrupt traditional business models, financial institutions should figure out new formulas to add practical value. In many instances, successful digital value propositions will require embedding a combination of financial products as an underlying service.

By tapping a vibrant ecosystem of digital innovators and service providers, even the nimblest credit union will be able to develop an active market presence and digital offerings. In such an integrated value chain, highly adaptable, seamless end-to-end processing at digital speed will be essential.

What role will financial institutions play in the digital ecosystem? It will depend on their simultaneous ability to catch up with the digital pace and evolve their strategic business leadership. Those institutions that adopt cloud technologies to interconnect and partner with digital service providers will attain a position of privilege and gain a competitive edge.

DIGITAL IDENTITY AND PRIVACY

This book describes disruptive changes underway in the financial services industry. It is imperative to remember that many of these changes have implications for human rights, privacy, and identity. There has been massive growth in the amount and nature of the data about individuals that is gathered by financial institutions and digital providers. Many new data sources feed into the creation of what we call *financial identities*. One basic example of a financial identity is seen in credit scoring, in which many data points and sources are used to make judgments about people.

Fintechs and other digital providers peer deeper into the lives of people. Many new services seek to increase the scope and nature of the data gathered about individuals. Data that people would consider as having nothing to do with the financial sphere, such as their text messages or social media posts, is being used at an increasing rate and, yet, the appropriate protections are either weak or absent.

Also, the nature of decision making within financial services is changing. Whereas the power of AI and machine learning to make decisions are being utilized, the understanding of the consequences and dangers of these technologies are lagging. New forms of crime, discrimination, and other attacks to civil rights may yet arise as a result. Financial institutions, digital providers, and governments will need to come together and orchestrate concerted actions and policies to protect personal identity and privacy.

2.
VALUE IN A DIGITAL WORLD

THE DIGITAL MIND

SINCE THE ONSET OF THE twenty-first century, humanity has been experiencing the progressive blurring of the lines that set apart physical and digital interactions. As electronic gadgets, ubiquitous connectivity, and online services pervade our day-to-day physical existence, the *born digital* generations take the comingling of these interactions quite naturally.

Being wired comes naturally to millennials. They are always connected and communicate digitally with friends and work colleagues. millennials cherish indistinct access to work and leisure from virtually any remote location or a designated physical office. Their work-life balance hinges on a continuum of business and personal interactions.

Some people thrive in a new breed of digital experiences. Many individuals feel more comfortable spending their time connected through digital services rather than mingling with humans. Gamers are a typical example, as they have played in a digital world since their early childhood.

Relentless technology advances are impacting human nature and society at large. The World Economic Forum highlighted the dawn of a fourth Industrial Revolution (Davis, 2016) as "a new era that builds and extends the impact of digitization in new and unanticipated ways."

Navigating the next industrial revolution

Revolution		Year	Information
⚙	1	1784	Steam, water, mechanical production equipment
💡	2	1870	Division of labour, electricity, mass production
🖥	3	1969	Electronics, IT, automated production
🧠	4	?	Cyber-physical systems

Exhibit 1 – Navigating the next industrial revolution
Source: World Economic Forum

Exhibit 1 highlights the earlier industrial revolutions. Mechanical equipment automated many of the manual labor tasks, electricity gave rise to mass production industries, and a combination of electronics and computer processing rounded up the automation journey. What is next? Thanks to a growing share of digital capabilities in this new cyber-physical world, individual activities will become increasingly specialized. And more people will begin to value digital interactions above and beyond their widespread praise for material things, such as physical goods and services.

As reflected in the International Telecommunications Union (ITU) statistical report *Measuring the Information Society* (ICT

Statistics, 2018), the world population has grown at a moderate clip of 1.2 percent annually between 2007 and 2018. Meanwhile, the number of users connected to the internet has kept climbing at a hefty compound annual growth rate (CAGR) of 10.8 percent, which represents a 9 times faster pace.

And the penetration of internet services globally went from 19.7 percent of the total population to 53.3 percent.

As shown in the report chart and added table of *Exhibit 2,* the spectacular surge in *high-speed mobile* users between 2012 and 2016, and its continuing rise, will enable a ubiquitous and increasingly universal access to digital services.

People (billions)	2007	2018	CAGR
Total world population	6.6	7.5	1.2%
Internet users	1.3	4.0	10.8%
Internet penetration	**19.7%**	**53.3%**	

Chart 1.14: Mobile coverage by type of network, 2007–2018*

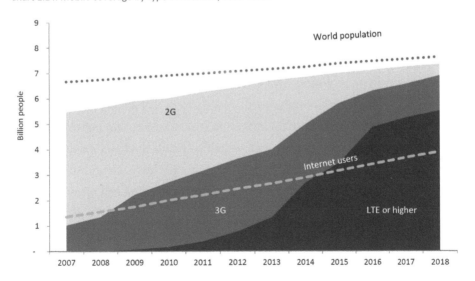

Note: * ITU estimate.
Source: ITU.

Exhibit 2 – Mobile coverage by type of network, 2007–2018
Source: International Telecommunications Union (ITU)

DIGITAL BRAINPOWER?

Since humanity learned how to harness the power of domestic animals, engineering, technology, and the perception of speed and time has been accelerating from the paced experience of walking to riding, then to trains, cars, and airplanes. Most recently, the born digital generations are taking for granted the prowess of advanced technologies. As human perception copes with a constant flurry of digital stimuli, our brain is evolving to higher levels of cognition.

Brainpower is demonstrating plenty of capacity to extend far beyond the slow and sequential physical interactions to the fast and concurrent digital swarm of the modern world. Perception occurs through all our senses. At a foundational level, our brain can discern sounds and get us to visualize a focused set of objects and learn to identify basic patterns.

Then the brain would drive suitable and timely responses to a wide range of stimuli, to include our own emotions and thoughts. Rapid successions of visual stimuli, as well as our peripheral vision, can trigger broader and deeper levels of perception. It is the same with the brain's ability to reason and spark internal stimuli derived from our own profound insights and thoughts.

So, our brain has come to grips with stimuli received when walking or riding a vehicle, and ultimately, when staring out of a fast-moving plane or spaceship. Lately, the sub-second speeds of virtual navigation through vast amounts of data, text, and images has compounded the challenge to the brain. New digital gimmicks, like live holograms and mixed reality, will bring the digital world much closer to the physical.

What happens to our sense of time when we operate at digital speeds? It is worth paraphrasing one of the concepts stemming from Einstein's theory of special relativity (Einstein, 1905): for two observers, moving at pronouncedly different speeds, their time clocks would tick at a different pace.

DIGITAL PERCEPTION

By analogy, the perception of time may work quite differently for physical-digital interactions. For single-threaded physical interactions occurring at a gentle human pace, time elapses slowly—much slower than the hasty and intense digital thrill of plunging into high-performance multiplayer games.

The impact of digital stimuli on human emotions is also noticeable. Emotions may span a broad spectrum encompassing multiple states, from love to hate, from trust to fear, from solace to stress, and from pleasure to pain. At a foundational level, digital stimuli may reach to our primal reflexes. However, an unstoppable tsunami of divergent digital stimuli and information may strain our ability to respond in the spur of the moment, thus triggering feelings and responses, such as anxiety and irrational urge.

The virality of peculiar visuals and sounds may also trigger complex feelings and responses. Feelings may ride on pre-established social network relationships and belongingness to affinity groups. Instant reactions (e.g., like and dislike) and comments validate and amplify these feelings. In such comingling of physical and digital interactions, a flood of concurrent digital facts may appear as the primary source of the truth and even override the perception of physical realities.

DIGITAL ASSETS

Market capitalization serves as a comparative gauge of how much investors appreciate a given company, sector, or peer group. Particularly when taking a long-term view that makes abstraction from continual stock market fluctuations and periodic corporate actions.

Exhibit 3 depicts the market capitalization of selected companies as derived from their respective values at the end of each year between 2008 and 2019 (Wolfram|Alpha, 2020). Interestingly, the value of the selected digital players (in this example, Apple, Microsoft, and Amazon) has appreciated steadily during this period at a robust CAGR of 25.3 percent, which dwarfs the market performance of traditional sectors such as banking (example of J.P. Morgan Chase) and consumer goods (example of Procter and Gamble).

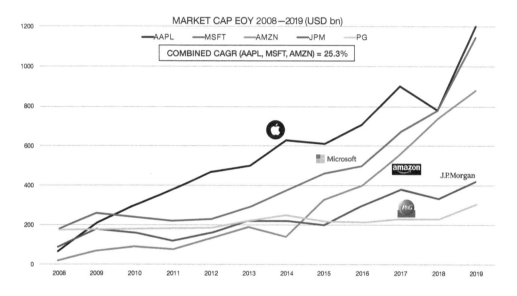

Exhibit 3 – Market capitalization of selected companies 2008–2019
Data source: Wolfram\Alpha

The comparative higher value that investors may attribute to digital players would in part reward their sustained and stronger growth. Investors weigh key indicators such financial performance, market expansion, and innovation in products and services. Still, an underlying factor stands out: digital players are creating new types of value.

Indeed, the underlying thrust of this brave new sector stems from the growing customer appreciation and demand for digital products and services such as software, personalized and social interactions, real-time information, instant, intelligent, and ubiquitous access, and digital media content.

Therefore, the value of digital products and services, as perceived by customers, is at least as tangible (or even higher) than what has been attached to traditional physical goods and services. Whereas most physical objects and services would cater primarily to the lower echelons in the hierarchy of human needs (Maslow, 1943), their digital counterparts seem to appeal to higher needs and wants such as belongingness and love, esteem, or self-actualization.

Hence, such special digital value will drive massive demand for enjoyable life experiences and sustain global economic growth. Global participation in producing and delivering digital value will help in expanding economic activity. However, people who lack access to digital broadband connectivity may suffer and nagging inequality indicators could deteriorate further.

BLURRING THE PHYSICAL AND DIGITAL WORLDS

How will the growing appetite for digital interactions affect companies and human behavior? For starters, the separation between the physical and digital worlds is blurring out. Or better, the combination of physical and digital interactions is sparking new flashes of value. For example, smartphones serve as a mobile physical gateway to a universe of digital services.

Mobile payments services have turned the smartphone into a most convenient and secure physical form factor. And smartphones encapsulate personal attributes and distinctive features, such as location and identity, that bring special value to the digital interactions. Photography and movies have been digital for a while. Selfies and mobile video chat are examples of smartphone interactivity. Digital music, movies, gaming, TV, and digital services can be consumed on the spot and by the drink.

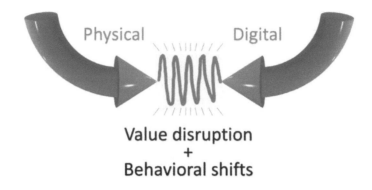

Value disruption
+
Behavioral shifts

Exhibit 4 – Blurring and combination of physical and digital interactions

As sketched in *Exhibit 4,* concurrent outcomes of combining physical and digital interactions include the disruption of the traditional value chain and shifts in human behavior. Such comingling comes naturally to millennials or the born digital generations and whets their appetites for multi-threading interactions and instant rewards.

Artificial intelligence may augment individual intellect, decision making, and operating capacity. Hence the creation of new physical-digital value. Personalized attention powered by intelligent, holistic digital services will provide customers with a superior experience. In contrast to the traditional physical value chains, the number of digital providers may scale up rapidly and significantly. And competition between large players, old and new, may heat up abruptly.

Behemoth companies such as Amazon stand out by combining digital and physical value. Their aim is to pervade all customer interactions, marketplace services, payments, and finance, typically through a combination of online orders and courier delivery or pick-up at stores. Amazon's massive capacity to acquire customer transactions, coupled with its combined digital and physical distribution network and aggregate services, caters to the everyday and lifetime customer needs.

As forces such as customer loyalty and market share prevail, financial services institutions must evolve their business models to compete effectively and catch up with the advances in digital distribution, marketing, and customer experience. Digital competition will open any customer base that was deemed to be captive or loyal.

ACCELERATING WITH DIGITAL SPEED

In the digital world, value creation may accrue much faster than with traditional goods and services. And the number of physical interactions may scale up many more times, possibly by two orders of magnitude.

Figure 2 – Immersed in the digital world

A comparative analysis of typical cash flows may illustrate this point. For example, in settling the exchange of value for traditional goods and services the lapse between financial inflows and outflows may span days (cash), a few months (short-term financing), or several years (long-term financing). In contrast, digital value may also embed subjective, short-lived components that get activated on the spot, such as enhanced real options, quality of decisions, and perceived gratification.

Such digital value components only live in the spur of the moment and may get traded instantly. For such exchange of value, variables like intensity, outreach, and velocity may tick with digital speed and pervasive interconnectivity—to the point of virality. And the aggregate value of a given digital feature or service may spike exponentially in a matter of minutes.

Unintended consequences of the unfettered growth of the digital value chain may stoke volatility and systemic instability in financial markets. Basically, because the ephemeral nature of digital fancy and fashion may affect corporate cash flows, market traction, and their resulting valuations.

Trading of digital assets and derivative securities in secondary markets may exacerbate the issue much further. Financial markets struggle to valuate the surges in unfettered digital interactions and cash flows. Excessive leverage may create potential imbalances and significant downside exposure. *Exhibit 5* highlights key forces at play in such a compressed, massive, and potentially leveraged digital cycle.

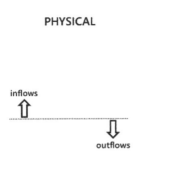

PHYSICAL

- Short-term and long-term
- Constrained flow of physical goods and services
- Steady, tangible value

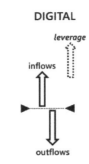

DIGITAL

- Compressed, instant cycle
- Frictionless flows
- Multiplied and subjective value

Exhibit 5 – Shorter cycles and leverage in the digital value chain

Most traditional financial services institutions are challenged to adapt to the real-time speed, spikes, and swings of digital markets and customer needs. Some are still mired in old-fashioned operating cultures, with fractured processes, manual steps, and dated technologies. Whereas born digital customers demand immediate response, twenty-four hours a day, seven days a week. And employees servicing transactions such as loans, payments, and investments, struggle to operate at digital speeds.

Highly profitable hedge funds thrive on business models that ride on algorithmic trading. However, in a digital world encompassing massive and global capital markets, the economic value of high frequency trading will be harder to justify.

The argument that microsecond arbitration would supply extra liquidity to smoothen market spikes might not hold water in massive digital markets. Why? Market spikes may arise out of sudden distress or merely because of the herd mindset of financial firms.

Contrarian and arbitrage trading strategies may add instant value and muffle the spikes. Conversely, when anybody can trade using diverse intelligent agents the global battle would shift to algorithms and speed. Should algorithms align massively and perversely, they may stoke market spikes and exacerbate swings and volatility.

DIGITAL CRISES

In our freewheeling digital universe, the actual truth is becoming much harder to discern. A giant wave of data and commentary from uncontested sources may rush in continually. And people lack a reasonable time to absorb such a multitude of facts, skewed factoids, and sheer misinformation.

Two millennia, filled with paced discourse and reflection, have elapsed since ancient Rome was ruled by its senate. In that ancient age information moved slowly, mostly by word-of-mouth. Oratory and prolonged debate in the Roman Senate would settle the law of the land. It took a long time for rulers to act upon the changing circumstances or respond to external challenges.

Change did happen anyhow, albeit oftentimes in a dramatic fashion. In his vehement speech to the Roman Senate, Consul Marcus Tullius Cicero denounced a conspiracy to overthrow his republic. Emboldened by his persuasive rhetoric, Cicero exclaimed: "Oh, what times! Oh what customs!" This was his famous Latin expression, "O tempora o mores" (Cicero, 63 B.C.). His powerful discourse curtailed the uprising.

Modern customs indeed, or a potpourri of unrestricted manners, are mutating dramatically in the digital age. Digital data swells as an information tsunami that disrupts traditional business models and thought processes and creates new decision and discernment paradigms. Opposite a customary depth and diversity of opinion with constructive point counterpoint debate, the digital information swell begets a scroll-through, blip-of-time decision culture.

Social networks are plagued with thousands, even millions, of one-click *likes* along with favorable and unfavorable commentary. Collective digital sentiment builds up virally, as millions of people cast their verdicts. Volatile consensus in social networks results in instant fame and fade, viral favor or condemnation, and universal popularity or panic.

ENDLESS DIGITAL INFORMATION

At the onset of today's digital times, the overabundance of information had already become an issue. In his book *Brave New World Revisited*, Aldous Huxley reflected about our ability to comprehend when he said, "But life is short and information endless: Nobody has time for everything" (Huxley, 1958).

The information tsunami has compounded this unstructured search and comprehension challenge. Information spreads out across myriad sources which may contradict, rather than reaffirm, one another. In a fast-paced digital world people get overwhelmed by so much information. Notwithstanding the help of intelligent search engines, people still may hardly find exactly what they need in a timely manner.

In the business and financial world, the mushrooming complexity of data and widespread interconnectedness is creating both formidable opportunities and unforeseen vulnerabilities. For instance, financial services institutions must process, record, and retain growing quantities of unstructured data, such as chats and social media interactions, along with exploding amounts of digital media, transaction records, and interactions.

Discovering relevant insights amid the couple thousand petabytes of structured and unstructured data that get created every day (Marr, 2018) becomes a daunting processing challenge. Mining and acting upon such rich sources of information in quasi real-time will serve as a mighty factor for competitive advantage.

With the hyperscale power of cloud computing, state-of-the-art artificial intelligence techniques will navigate such massive amounts of information effectively and swiftly. Feeding and training deep-learning models with selected chunks of unstructured data may create an underlying layer of *learned intelligence*. This intrinsic level of intelligence will provide organizations a most valuable digital asset derived from massive data.

In May 2020, Microsoft announced its AI Supercomputer, built in collaboration with the Open AI organization. It is hosted in the Azure cloud and was designed to train artificial intelligence models. Its large computing power will facilitate training models for natural language processing, computer vision, and other perceptual domains. "The exciting thing about these models is the breadth of things they're going to enable," said Microsoft Chief Technical Officer Kevin Scott (Microsoft Corporation, 2020).

DIGITAL BLACK HOLES

Besides having to navigate and process unwieldy amounts of data, global hyper-connectivity is creating a big nightmare for most organizations. A continuing rise in cyberattacks aims at vulnerabilities in any part of a complex and growing global array of networks and software. Given the hefty financial and reputational damage inflicted by cybercrime, many organizations are waking up to the need to manage a new and multilateral cyber-dimension of risk.

The financial services value chain, to include banks, credit unions, securities firms, and corporations, moves money and other financial assets electronically, and is a frequent cybercrime target. To provide an effective level of defense, the financial sector must team up with advanced cybersecurity organizations. In a nutshell: the best approach to protect against organized cybercrime is to get better organized and build global cybersecurity capabilities.

In this interconnected digital world, safeguarding personal information is a major exposure in terms of data protection and privacy. Besides the direct financial damage from cyberattacks, regulators globally are holding companies accountable for data and privacy breaches. For example, the General Data Protection Regulation (The European Parliament and the Coucil of the European Union, 2016) has been enforced since May 25, 2018, and carries multimillion-dollar fines. And beyond the perils of financial and identity theft, individuals are also exposed to orchestrated and viral cyberbullying.

Despite stringent controls by companies, organizations, and social networks, the decentralized nature of the interconnected digital world may allow for *any-to-any* interaction schemes. How will individuals and corporations feel secure and establish relationships of digital trust in such context? Could it be with anybody or everybody? That would seem most unlikely! Perhaps in leading transnational corporations and multinational entities? Only in a select few ... Then which ones? In today's cyber-universe, the underlying challenge is to distinguish digital good from evil.

DIGITAL DOOMSDAY SCENARIOS

The proliferation of digital services across borders will have an increasing impact on international trade. A relentless growth in the monetary sector, as well as the intangible value of digital services, will gain more significance within the cross-border payments for goods and services.

As illustrated in *Exhibit 6*, imports of goods and services in advanced economies have been inching up at a CAGR of 3.2 percent between 2006 and 2018. For emerging economies, imports have grown at a comparatively higher CAGR of 7.1 percent over the same period. It is important to notice how this higher growth in imports affects the balance of payments in emerging economies.

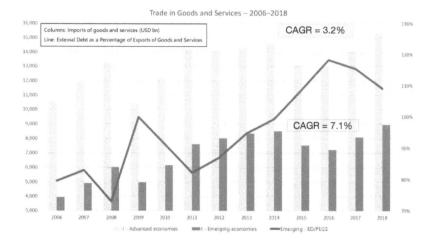

Exhibit 6 – Global growth in imports versus external debt
Source: International Monetary Fund—World Economic
Outlook Database

The line in the chart reflects the external debt of emerging economies as a percentage of exports of goods and services. Over the same period, this debt percentage climbed from 80 percent to 109 percent, which hints at an imbalance. Opposite a significant growth in imports, exports from emerging economies seem to have a hard time offsetting the buildup in external debt. An increasing net flow of digital services originating from advanced economies may continue to strain this imbalance. So, emerging economies need to play a more active role as exporters in the high-growth field of digital services.

A rise in external debt, coupled with the global tsunami of digital services, unstructured data, and cyber-vulnerabilities, may spark another financial crisis. The aggregate value of net flows of digital assets, both in services and content, will gain cross-border significance.

Particularly for emerging economies that are net digital importers. And instant digital fashion plus virality may cause uncontrollable spikes in demand.

In a doomsday scenario, digital financing (and securitization) may amplify a sudden increase in the debt levels and financial leverage. Given the asymmetry between digital debt and digital assets, a sudden drop in asset values could become catastrophic. What will happen when the high-flying global demand for digital services and content being sourced from emerging economies stalls or nosedives?

Lacking a standard approach to determine the valuation of distressed digital assets, their value could plummet. Investor panic and dwindling consumer confidence might end up erasing much of their value. And the volatility of cryptocurrencies backing digital assets might aggravate the situation. Facing a steep downward spiral in digital asset values, the surge in digital debt and leverage may escape the controls and stability provisions of the financial sector. Hence, an unprecedented, devastating crisis might unfold.

DIGITAL RESPONSE TO A KILLER COVID-19 VIRUS?

What about the impact of a pernicious pandemic such as COVID-19? In February 2020, digital media propagated a visceral fear of this killer disease, as well as misinformation about it, faster than what the time it took the coronavirus to infect the entire world. An intertwined international travel network, coupled with the unprecedented contagion of this nasty virus, ended up paralyzing most of the world. The toll of the number of deaths and economic malaise turned out to be devastating.

The only effective public health defense at hand was to shut down non-essential economic activity and keep people at home, in self-quarantine. Spiked with continual waves of scary digital news, the global shutdown wreaked havoc in financial markets.

Through forty bearish and volatile days that began on February 12, 2020, unyielding financial panic pushed down the Dow-Jones Industrial

Average (DJIA) index, which ended up dropping 37 percent from its peak. In such a distressed scenario, how can financial institutions establish the value of assets and forecast economic activity?

The short answer is that most deterministic models fail to accommodate the stark realities and unpredictability that prevails in distressed scenarios. However, positive mitigation and rapid cures will always remain as practical defenses. In the financial world, defensive weapons pivot on special credit facilities coupled with central injections of liquidity.

BECOMING DIGITAL

At the end of the day, the onus will rest with banks and credit unions to grant financial assistance to strained customers and members. Many financial institutions face the challenge of adapting existing credit policies, administrative procedures, and technology systems fast enough to forestall a major and irreversible breakdown, as well as addressing the limitations to open and operate physical branches. Given the disruption of regular corporate life, how can financial executives navigate the harsh realities, arrive at effective decisions, and mobilize their organizations to action?

A well-orchestrated digital response may come to the rescue. The number one pillar will be an enterprise-wide, secure collaboration platform that allows financial services personnel to work remotely. Second, the pervasive enablement of digital channels such as home banking, mobile banking, and institutional presence in social media will be imperative.

Next, advanced cybersecurity is needed to fend off bad actors— domestic and foreign—that seek to exploit the pandemic distress and the inherent vulnerabilities of the digital world. Finally, the adoption of authentication methods such as electronic signature wherever it complies with existing regulations must be implemented.

In summary, institutions that attain the most progress in combining their physical operations with digital technologies will be able to respond faster and deliver the most value to their clients, customers, and members. Blending enterprise collaboration tools with everyday administrative and managerial workflows will result in much better and effective preparedness against viral attacks, whether from a natural or digital source. Rapid alignment across the organization, plus the ability to quickly digest conflicting information and reconfigure the digital operations, followed by concerted institutional response, will constitute the best remedies against unprecedented and unexpected threats.

REFERENCES

Cicero. (63 B.C.). First Oration Against Catiline. Orations Against Catiline. Rome, Roman Empire: Senate of the Roman Republic.

Davis, N. (2016, January 16). What is the fourth industrial revolution. Retrieved from World Economic Forum: https://www.weforum.org/agenda/2016/01/what-is-the-fourth-industrial-revolution/

Einstein, A. (1905). Zur Electrodynamik bewegter Korper. Annalen der Physik, 891-921.

Huxley, A. (1958). Brave New World Revisited. New York, NY: Harper and Brothers.

ICT Statistics. (2018). Measuring the Information Society Report. Retrieved from International Telecommunications Union: https://www.itu.int/en/ITU-D/Statistics/Pages/publications/misr2018.aspx

Marr, B. (2018, May 21). How Much Data Do We Create Every
        Day? The Mind-Blowing Stats Everyone Should Read.
        Retrieved from Forbes: https://www.forbes.com/sites/
        bernardmarr/2018/05/21/how-much-data-do-we-create-
        every-day-the-mind-blowing-stats-everyone-should-
        read/#2b4aae860ba9

Maslow, A. (1943). A Theory of Human Motivation. Psychological
        Review, American Psychological Association.

Microsoft Corporation. (2020, May 19). A.I. Supercomputer. Re-
        trieved from The AI Blog: https://blogs.microsoft.com/ai/
        openai-azure-supercomputer/

The European Parliament and the Coucil of the European Union.
        (2016). REGULATION (EU) 2016/679 (General Data
        Protection Regulation). Official Journal of the European
        Union, I. 119/1-88.

Wolfram|Alpha. (2020, May). Wolfram|Alpha computational
        intelligence. Retrieved from Wolfram|Alpha: https://www.
        wolframalpha.com/

3.
GENERATIONAL CHANGES

HOW ANCIENT CIVILIZATIONS
LEARNED TO LEARN

IN THE TIMES OF ANCIENT Greece, few scientific instruments were available and those in existence had limited observational capabilities. Hence, notable philosophers had to rely on deep thinking to conceptualize the nature of the universe or evaluate the evolution of humanity and society.

Plato was born in the Athens region in about 428 BC. Building on the thoughts of Socrates, he developed a profound system of philosophy. In about 387 BC Plato founded the Academy, a thought school for philosophers that also extended to mathematics and rhetoric (Encyclopaedia Britannica, Inc., 1995).

One of his students, Aristotle, ended up dissenting with Plato and established his own school, known as the Lyceum. Aristotle gathered around him a group of brilliant research students, called *peripatetics.* This student denomination came from the name of the Lyceum cloister (in Greek: *peripatos*) that contained walkways and colonnades, in which they walked and held their discussions. The legend is that Aristotle had allegedly acquired a habit of perambulating while lecturing his students (Wikipedia, n.d.).

Figure 3 – Plato (428-347 BC)

These ancient learning practices were restricted to a small number of selected students and built on the thought leadership of a few philosophers and scholars. Such deep academic learning methods could not scale out.

Fast forward to present times, academia is still challenged to reach the entire world population and its social echelons. How would new digital technologies disrupt and transform human learning and thought processes?

DIGITAL AS THE NEW LEARNING SOURCE

Right in this new decade of 2020, and for future generations, born digital persons will stand out for their native digital habits. It is most appropriate to call them digital natives.

In stark contrast with the learning methods of traditional academia, digital natives are developing an aversion for the old school. They demand engaging content and narrative. Much like Aristotle's dissent with Plato, they dispute the established precepts: "Amicus Plato sed magis amica veritas," meaning: Plato is my friend, but the truth is a better friend (Wikipedia, n.d.).

Digital content continues to explode. Digital natives must cope with an overabundance of rapidly changing information, sources, and different points of view. Their livelihood is connected to digital devices, and their minds crave digital stimuli. Increasingly intelligent apps draw their attention continually and effectively and augment their ingenuity. They find digital methods as the natural means to pull online content and interact with everyday friends, family members, and colleagues. They share feelings, photos, and thoughts, or simply tap digital media for their own introspection.

Up until the COVID-19 pandemic forced classrooms to become digital, schools were slow to adapt to the new realities. Most schools were stuck in a staid, old-fashioned classroom experience. In stark contrast, digital natives cherish high-speed online tutorials within a fleeting digital entourage.

In the past, learning was anchored in the paced personal rapport and knowledge transfer with an educator or parent. When compared to the freewheeling digital interactions with friends and online services in today's constantly online society, such pace seems awfully slow. Most teenagers are increasingly at odds with the traditional high-school learning environment. What will be the new paradigm for the youth to learn, mature, and live a productive life?

DIGITAL PSYCHE

Digital natives spend a good part of their time clicking, chatting, and typing, as well as listening to music, playing games, or watching content on a digital device. For some digital natives, such interaction patterns may become addictive. The global availability of exciting digital content, news, and relationships may extend the time online into the wee hours of the night.

In extreme cases, the urge to be constantly connected (or *wired*) may turn into a harmful pathology of the digital psyche. Digital addicts would spend more hours on a device, encroaching on healthy sleep time, than doing physical activities. Excessive immersion into the digital world may give rise to attention deficit disorders or unwieldy social behaviors.

Digital devices are replacing the rapport with human instructors and mentors. Computers are standing in as digital push button role models. In this digital learning mode, the locus of control is going through a reversal paradox: learners, instead of educators, have the upper hand to control the interaction. No wonder why conduct in class is facing new challenges.

A pervasive flow of instant messages and social media content rapidly disseminate even the most controversial factoids and charged opinions. Opinions get shared and augmented in digital media and acquire a sense of authenticity.

Many youngsters, being more gullible or naïve, may mistakenly believe fringe and weird opinions from odd and questionable sources to be true. Hence, baseless platitudes that challenge the status quo would resonate with younger generations and gain astounding popularity.

A perverse combination between a flurry of digital interactions, changing mode of control, and emergence of referential credibility in social media build up into a devastating force. It is causing a dire and damaging impact on the behavioral traits and awareness of broader interpersonal skills, manners, and civic awareness of digital natives.

It is high time that new learning methods of the digital world blended in many classic principles. People and society have been operating effectively for centuries.

Fortunately, the human brain has enormous potential to absorb large quantities of new information and context. And the brain functions have an innate ability to adapt to the dynamic digital stimuli and modes of interaction.

Individuals will learn to thrive in the digital environment. And their very physical nature and constitution may be affected too. The stakes of blending digital with traditional education are high. Like many other aspects of human evolution, the new digital psyche will be transmitted to future generations right at birth, both as parental influence and genetic traits.

DIGITAL FINANCIAL BEHAVIORS

Besieged by continual and simultaneous stimuli, the brains of digital natives, toddlers, children, and adolescents may develop a peculiar reasoning style. For example, making instant decisions primarily by analogy and appeal rather than dedicating effort and time to analyze or quantify. Or, in the case of most teenagers, as their brains complete the final development stages, and they tend to perfect their reasoning by experimenting with a contrarian (and sometimes seemingly illogical or rebel) posture.

What will digital natives want financial services for? Answering this question adequately will fundamentally reshape the industry strategy. Most likely, their income streams will be more volatile and less predictable than those of their parents. Their diminishing interest to stay in a job, their aversion to expensive and taxing long-term credit products, fear of risky investments, or their inclination to rent versus buy, will bring structural shifts to the economy.

Notwithstanding many appealing financial offerings, digital

natives would rather stay in control than depend on a financial institution to manage their monies. Right at their fingertips, they prefer buying lifestyle products and services from a creative ecosystem of digital providers. And instant financial orchestration may merely become a means to such ends.

Financial institutions will need to rethink the products and services that are relevant to this market segment. Providing person-to-person instant payments transactions, or the ability to share consumption bills are examples of such needs-based services. The end game seems to hinge on holistic partnerships across industry sectors. Helping digital natives build and manage their financial capacity will pivot on orchestrating the right combination of financial and non-financial products that they want.

THIS IS AMERICA!

Incredibly—and thanks to increased life spans—at least six distinct generations live side-by-side in the United States today.

Figure 4 – New workforce in America

Over time, these so-called demographic cohorts have earned the following names based on how they behave and the historical events that influenced them (Sievewright, 2019):

- The Lost Generation (1883–1900) describes the cohort who grew up in the period of the late imperialistic era and fought in World War I.
- The G.I. Generation (1901–1924) includes those who lived through WWI in their younger years. They had to master the Great Depression and fought in World War II and are also called the Greatest Generation.
- The Traditionalists (1925–1945) includes most of those who were born or growing up during the Great Depression and World War II, and who fought the Korean War. Also called the silent generation, or silents, because they were socialized at a time of conformity to authority. They saw the advent of TV!
- The Baby Boomers (1946–1964) got their name from the baby boom following World War II. They are a large demographic cohort and, due to the long time span, are sometimes separated into two groups: early boomers (1946–1955) and late boomers (1956–1964). They grew up during the early Cold War era with the Cuban Missile Crisis and the Vietnam War, and witnessed the moon landing, the civil and women's rights movements, and the arrival of color TV!
- Generation X or Gen X (1965–1980), the *baby bust* generation characterized by a drop in birth rates. They experienced the fall of the Berlin Wall and lifting of the iron curtain in Eastern Europe. Technologically, they saw the advent of the Walkman, the VCR and personal computers (IBM PC, Macintosh, etc.).
- Millennials, or Generation Y (1981–1994) grew up during the dot-com boom and enjoyed the turn of the millennium. Being mostly the offspring of the demographically large

baby boomers, they are the largest cohort. They have seen major technological shifts such as the advent of the internet, mobile phones, email, and text as well as advanced gaming consoles (Playstation, Xbox, etc.).

- Post-millennials, or Generation Z (1995–2010) grew up with smartphones, tablets, social media (Facebook, Google, Twitter, Snapchat, etc.) and mobile apps.

SELLING TO DIGITAL NATIVES

An interesting marketing strategy is to reach digital natives with tailored financial offerings to be presented through their parents. Initially offered as practical initiation in the financial world, they include products that could connect to the child and grow to a fully detached relationship once the child is of age. In the US, a generation of baby boomers will likely transfer over $30 billion of wealth to their children.

Despite the overabundance of online financial offerings, digital natives seem to lack a deeper understanding of how financial instruments work. A future challenge would be to provide practical tools to digital natives to educate their children on how to manage their finances and do business in the digital world in a manner that blends seamlessly with their lifestyle needs. *Exhibit 7* shows that younger generations will need a different breed of financial products that operate in a digital environment.

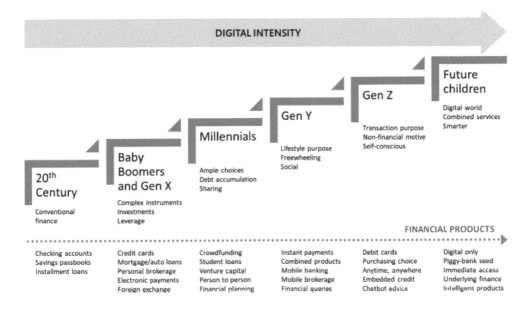

Exhibit 7 – Evolution of financial behaviors and products

HOW WILL GEN Z BEHAVE FINANCIALLY?

Much is understood and communicated about millennials and financial services. Whereas millennials are showing a healthy appetite for auto loans and card debt, they are saddled with almost half of the country's student loan debt. According to the Federal Reserve Bank of New York, total student loan debt in the US rose to $1.51 trillion by December 2019, with 9.2 percent transitioning into serious delinquency.

Conversely, strategies and theories are just emerging regarding Gen Z. As Gen Zers start to enter adulthood, many financial institutions are wondering what this generation wants in terms of financial services. How they will choose to borrow? At what pace would they adopt credit cards and personal loans to get on the first rung of the credit ladder?

Gen Z is the fastest-growing generation of borrowers

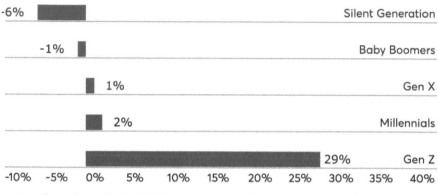

Annual growth rate (Q2 2018–Q2 2019) in number of consumers carrying a balance

Source: TransUnion Q2 2019

Exhibit 8 – Gen Z is the fastest-growing generation of borrowers
Source: TransUnion

Research shows that Gen Z already carries around 5 percent of US general purpose credit card debt and the same with auto loans. The dramatic growth of credit balances among Gen Z consumers was the fastest of all generations in the past year.

Exhibit 8 shows that, according to the TransUnion's Industry Insights Report, Gen Z consumers grew overall credit balances by 29 percent in the second quarter of 2019 from the same quarter in 2018. In comparison, the silent generation and boomers were declining in their overall debt load. This a clear indication that Gen Z consumers differ from millennials, who delayed the uptake of financial products such as credit cards, auto loans, and mortgages.

The important thing financial institutions need to know about selling credit products to Gen Z is that they are a mobile-first generation, unlike millennials who were an online-first generation.

This means that the expectations of how loans and credit cards are sold needs to meet with their mobile-first expectations. Anything short of an Uber app-like experience will turn away Gen Z prospective customers.

THE RISE AND RISE OF MULTI-GENERATIONAL HOUSEHOLDS

The United States is currently experiencing a sustained, decades-long growth in multi-generational households, according to recent research. Today, up to 41 percent of Americans who are buying a home are also considering accommodating a family customer from another generation, such as an elderly parent or adult child.

The number and share of Americans living in multi-generational family households have continued to rise (despite improvements in the US economy since the Great Recession). In 2016, a record 64 million people, or 20 percent of the US population, lived with multiple generations under one roof, based on analysis of census data.

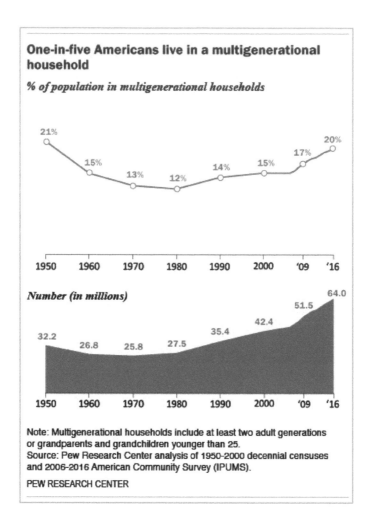

One-in-five Americans live in a multigenerational household

% of population in multigenerational households

Figure 5 – Americans living in multi-generational households

Multi-generational family living is growing among nearly all US racial groups, most age groups, and both men and women. The share of the population living in this type of household—defined as including two or more adult generations or including grandparents and grandchildren younger than 25—declined from 21 percent in 1950 to a low of 12 percent in 1980.

Since then, growth in multi-generational living has exploded. The number and share of Americans living in these households increased sharply during and immediately after the Great Recession of 2007–2009. Today, more than 60 million Americans—19 percent of the US population—are part of multi-generational homes.

Growing racial and ethnic diversity in the US population helps explain some of the rise in multi-generational living. The Asian and Hispanic populations overall are growing more rapidly than others and are more likely to live in multigenerational family households. Another growth factor is that foreign-born immigrants are more likely than Americans born in the US to live with multiple generations of family.

DEMOGRAPHIC SHIFTS ARE NOT JUST AN AGE THING

The face of America is changing, and multicultural consumers are quickly becoming the major part of the expected growth in the US, now and in the future. Currently, there are more than 130 million multicultural Americans in the US and they account for 40 percent of the population. In fact, as reflected in *Table 1*, nearly all of the US population growth since 2000 has come from multicultural segments:

Multicultural Group	Population Growth	Growth 2000–2019	% of Total Growth
Non-Hispanic Whites	1,510,265	0.8%	3.2%
Hispanics	29,177,345	83%	61%
Non-Hispanic Blacks	6,443,658	19%	13%
Non-Hispanic Asian & Pacific Islanders	8,758,829	84%	18%

Table 1 – US Multicultural Population Growth
Source: Coopera Consulting

Younger age groups are made up from a more diverse population, while older age groups tend to be less diverse. This dramatic trend in ethnicity by generation will have deep implications for marketers in the years and decades to come.

Hispanics account for the largest multicultural segment at 19.6 percent, followed by non-Hispanic Blacks and non-Hispanic Asian and Pacific Islanders, respectfully. Virtually all the growth now and into the foreseeable future will emanate from these three groups. Hispanics have been the second fastest-growing population segment since 2000, showing 83 percent growth.

Furthermore, where they live today may not be where they will live tomorrow, and understanding the growth and migration trends where multicultural groups live is key for financial institutions to target them now and in the future.

Perhaps the best way to reach your Hispanic target audience is to understand them. Here are some insights:

- Family, culture, and heritage are important to US Hispanics
- Fifty-six percent of Spanish-speaking Hispanics are more loyal to companies who advertise in Spanish
- Hispanic users spend almost ten and a half hours per week on their smartphones
- They tend to watch more videos online (Netflix, Amazon Prime, Hulu, etc.) on their smartphones

THE WORKPLACE OF THE FUTURE

Technology has given young people an unprecedented degree of connectivity among themselves and with the rest of the population. That makes generational shifts more important and speeds up technological trends as well. For companies, this shift will bring both challenges and equally attractive opportunities.

By 2030, US organizations will face significant talent management challenges due to generational shifts in the labor market, such as:

- The first wave of baby boomers is already retiring, although the second wave of boomers (1955–1964) will still be a driving force in established organizations until the mid-2020s, when most of them will also leave the workplace
- Gen Xers will gradually rise to prominence in established companies threatened by the fast-changing, highly dynamic modern market environment, and lead the business side of start-ups together with emerging Gen Y leaders
- Millennials will gain strong influence and will start thinking and behaving more like those of previous generations but will define new leadership and cultural dynamics in the workplace
- Some of the chairs left behind by the retiring baby boomers (although not necessarily the ones in the corner offices) will be filled by Gen Zers starting their work lives

In addition to becoming the largest generation and consumer group, millennials are also reshaping organizations from the inside. To stay ahead in a rapidly changing market, financial institutions should do the same!

This demographic seeks opportunities that help them grow. They are interested in on-demand work, free-agency, and other ways to give themselves more skill growth, flexibility, and autonomy. Contrary to popular belief, millennials do not want to *company hop*—but rather they want to *job hop* within the same company. Financial institutions should take the opportunity to examine job responsibilities, organizational structures, and job leveling to look for ways to provide the type of stimulation they are seeking.

As digital natives, millennials have the technical skillsets businesses seek to stay ahead of the curve. They also bring unique perspectives to designing and improving products and services. This new type of thinking can help financial institutions reconsider how they develop products, service their customers, and balance technology solutions to keep innovating on behalf of their customers.

However, while millennials are still flooding into the workforce, representation at senior levels in many US companies often remains limited. According to Spencer Stuart, the average age of independent directors (board customers) for S&P 500 companies was close to sixty-three years old.

Financial institutions can still harness the value of millennial thinking without putting them on their board, by making concerted efforts to engage with them.

GENERATIONAL SHIFTS IN AN ON-DEMAND WORLD

Projected to grow to $335 billion by 2025, the *on-demand economy* has changed how we live, travel, and work. With millennials reluctant to commit to choices, such as owning a home, the on-demand economy provides this generation with the access that they are looking for, but not necessarily the burdens of a long-term commitment.

A car hailed, a room booked, a job filled—all at the swipe of a finger. This is the on-demand economy. Thanks to advancing technology and customers pushing for a better experience, old ways of doing business are being transformed. Also known as the *gig economy* and the *sharing economy*, this new economic model has become a phenomenon.

This on-demand world has some interesting metrics:

- Seventy-two percent of Americans have used some type of shared or on-demand online service
- Approximately 160 million people in Europe and the United States—or around 20 percent of the working population—

engage in some form of independent work

- Eighty-eight percent of millennials wish they could have greater opportunity to start and finish work at the times they choose

From transportation to accommodation to financial services, the on-demand model disrupts every sector it enters—and has also created new ones.

Even established firms are adding on-demand elements to their business models. US retail giant Walmart recently began building a network of on-demand delivery drivers from its own employees, to deliver customer orders on their way home.

WHAT DO SHIFTING DEMOGRAPHICS MEAN FOR INNOVATION?

Expect innovation to flourish when the pragmatic, creative, and entrepreneurial Gen Xers innovate alongside the collaborative, idealistic Gen Yers, supported by the fresh ideas of the flexible, multicultural, and balanced Gen Zers! Innovation focus will shift to meaningful emphasis from making money first to making meaning first. This is good news for financial institutions!

Once the remaining baby boomers fade off gradually from the workplace in the next decade, every employee will be a digital native. Powered by the advent of profound technological change, new technologies and related industries will emerge that will drive economic growth for the next two or three decades.

Looking forward, collaborative digital workplaces will emerge, possibly powered by virtual reality solutions that allow team customers to collaborate in real-time under the guidance of an innovation process expert.

With the gradual departure of the baby boomers from the C-suite of big corporations, the cultural transformation of many established corporations will be led by the more pragmatic, entrepreneurial, and creative Gen X leaders. Innovation will continue moving from the closed toward a more open paradigm as collaborative millennials and technology-addicted post-millennials will gradually gain more influence in the labor market.

WHAT DOES IT MEAN FOR FINANCIAL INSTITUTIONS?

As global connectivity soars, generational shifts could come to play a more important role in setting behavior than socioeconomic differences do. Young people have become a potent influence on people of all ages and incomes, as well as on the way those people consume and relate to brands.

An aging workforce, aging consumers, the shift in economic power, and the rise of the millennial generation (Gen Y) will have profound implications and opportunities for your financial institution. Companies will need to anticipate demographic developments and bring products and services into line with the changing customer base.

As people live longer and state support declines, the competitive frontline is likely to shift from lending toward helping people to fund and manage their retirements. Reputation and trust will be crucial in sustaining market share in an increasingly empowered and knowledgeable retirement market.

There are other important trends and factors that financial institutions will need to follow:

- Customers will reach financial institutions through an ever-expanding suite of channels and touchpoints. Financial institutions cannot afford to ignore the power of data and analytics. Those that leverage the power of big data and analytics into their operations will show productivity gains and profitability margins that are significantly higher than those of their peers.

- Fueling future growth will require an ever-increasing emphasis on digital channels: without significant prioritization of digital channel engagement, the ability to acquire and retain an increasingly digital consumer base will be more and more difficult.

- Personalized interaction will increasingly happen online instead of in branches, and just because a customer is opening an app and not the door of the branch does not mean that he or she expects inferior service. According to recent research, 33 percent of customers abandon business relationships because personalization is lacking and 73 percent of consumers expect specialized treatment for being a good customer.

Furthermore, research suggests that consumers will turn toward brands who listen and learn from their behaviors and who create genuine relationships with them.

As a theme, the increasing emphasis on meeting the needs of the consumers on their terms is hard to ignore. The great news for marketers, regardless of industry, is that the tools, data, and intelligence has come together to meet and exceed these expectations.

The key question financial institution leaders need to ask themselves is whether they are prepared for the next generations.

REFERENCES

Encyclopaedia Britannica, Inc. (1995). Plato and Platonism. In T. N. Britannica, *The New Encyclopaedia Britannica* (pp. Vol. 25, 893). Chicago: Encyclopaedia Britannica, Inc.

Sievewright, M. (2019). *Generations Next.* Sievewright & Associates.

Wikipedia. (n.d.). *Amicus Plato.* Retrieved from Wikipedia: https://en.wikipedia.org/wiki/Amicus_Plato,_sed_magis_amica_veritas

Wikipedia. (n.d.). *Peripatetic school.* Retrieved from Wikipedia: https://en.wikipedia.org/wiki/Peripatetic_school

4.
INTELLIGENT EXPERIENCES

DIGITAL DISRUPTION IS EVERYWHERE!

RAPID AND RELENTLESS ADVANCES OF novel technologies in consumer industries, typically consumer electronics, are influencing the behaviors and expectations of digital customers globally. The quest for the latest and greatest gadgets is stoking the fugacity of consumer preferences, marked by shorter cycles from fashion to fade.

Myriad digital interactions accelerate the pace of everyday life. As continual technology innovations swarm and ensnare humans, the psyches of digitally minded individuals are experiencing some visible shifts. As the brain adjusts to this swarm of digital stimuli, the span of human perception is also shifting. The brain learns to absorb more and at a faster rate, thus making the digital generation crave an endless series of deeper and shorter thrills.

"The biggest change in consumers' financial services needs and behaviors is unlikely to be around the types of products and services they use but, rather, in how they access, use, and manage them and—potentially—who they obtain them from" (Sievewright, Finding the Future - The World in 2030, 2017).

Figure 6 – Ladders to the Decade of 2030

Understanding the shifts in consumer behaviors will be a key success factor to prevail amid these rapid transformations. For example, institutions can gain relevant insights through direct interactions with consumers daily. Behavioral experts can dissect individual preferences for digital experiences by watching very closely how consumers react to innovations in products and services.

Nimble, consumer-oriented institutions seem to have a strategic advantage. Their close and constant contact with consumers may provide a fertile ground for experimenting on innovative features, functions, business models, and processes. Small and agile organizations can manage experimentation in a controlled scale and are better positioned to introduce rapid adjustments that maximize the creative impact, remove friction, and significantly improve the digital experience.

To develop and deliver end-to-end digital services, smaller institutions must pivot on external levers. Tapping the vibrant ecosystem of digital services and technology partners, smaller institutions can leapfrog ahead. Larger, incumbent players struggle to overcome legacy cultures, operations, and technologies and tend to compete using their own internal and proprietary resources.

"The well-defined and successfully executed digital strategies that many credit unions are progressing today will form the foundation for success tomorrow; and, the integration of digital technologies and capabilities into a credit union's 'eco-system'—in ways that create a compelling value system for members—will play a hugely significant role in determining whether a credit union survives and thrives or falls by the wayside" (Sievewright, Finding the Future - The World in 2030, 2017).

Digital disruption is everywhere and is creating new opportunities across all industry sectors. This is seen especially in financial services, where new entrants are challenging incumbents claiming the advantage in client, customer, and member experience through easy, fast, and frictionless interactions.

"For credit unions, the challenge is clear: get rid of the processes that are creating friction for your members and/or are slowing you down (in serving them better)" (Sievewright, Digital Transaction Management and Transformation, 2019).

AIMING HIGH WITH DIGITAL CUSTOMER EXPERIENCE

Renowned technology companies such as Amazon, Apple, and Netflix have set the customer experience bar very high. Regardless of how consumers choose to interact with them, the experience of working with most of these firms is usually outstanding.

To make the point about the customer experience focus, Amazon's

CEO, Jeff Bezos, once said: "You want to be customer obsessed, not competitor obsessed. Customers are always dissatisfied, and they always want more. If you're competitor obsessed and you're a leader, you see everyone behind you, and you slow down a bit. But customers pull you along."

Similarly, fintechs have made inroads into financial services by following other frictionless mantras. These companies are not only far more agile and innovative than most incumbents, but they know how to rapidly develop, smoothly operate, and successfully drive digital businesses.

However, many financial institutions can rise to the challenges posed. In researching the digital transformation strategies of financial institutions in Asia, Development Bank of Singapore (DBS) stands out. They rose to the digital challenge by embracing the changes going on around them and giving the fintech businesses a run for their money!

DBS realized that it needed to do more for its customers, and this led to the creation of its *R.E.D.* mantra: *R*espectful, *E*asy to deal with, and *D*ependable. The bank's COO—who championed the initiative—explained his thought process like this: "People's lives don't revolve around banking. If you're making a major purchase like buying a refrigerator, the smaller and faster the banking piece, the better. To make banking joyful, make the banking part invisible!"

THE FUTURE IS BOTH PHYSICAL AND DIGITAL

Bank branches and financial centers are also adapting to the digital world. It is not a question on whether branches will be either digital or physical, but more on how they can blend advanced capabilities from both digital and physical branch interaction models.

Real estate economics (bricks) will drive modern branches to eschew routine transactions that can be automated or performed better and more efficiently elsewhere. To thrive in the digital world, branches must become experiential, and provide more exciting reasons for a productive visit, to include friendly and focused relationships.

Branch banking is not dead; it is just evolving. Unquestionably, the financial services industry is going through the most significant transformation in its history: it is rapidly becoming digital. The reality is that consumers (and businesses) still prefer to conduct more sensitive, valuable, or complex transactions in-person. Why would people rather do so?

To put it simply, people need to trust their financial providers. And most customers, members, and clients appreciate the kind of advice and high-touch treatment that banks, credit unions, and investment advisors may deliver in-person.

For most financial institutions, the challenge is to establish a trusted rapport that would anchor a healthy relationship. A familiar, face-to-face, personalized tone plays an interesting role in keeping up this trusted rapport. After establishing the relationship in person, savvy financial institutions may carry on with trusted interactions in a virtual face-to-face mode using secure videoconferencing. A side effect of the COVID-19 pandemic was to rush the adoption of videoconferencing as a trusted channel.

Figure 7 – Trusted digital relationships

Technology advances are allowing institutions to conduct financial transactions through rich multimedia videoconferences. State-of-the-art videoconferencing sessions are bringing together consumers, account executives, documentation, and financial specialists in a most secure and auditable manner that complies with stringent industry regulations.

And artificial intelligence tools may augment the knowledge and effectiveness of these virtual face-to-face sessions. Concurrent speech recognition and understanding may track the conversation and inspire actionable recommendations that financial advisors can produce on the spot.

Internal chatbots may answer many queries about subtle features of diverse products and services instantly and precisely, which would otherwise have demanded some *we will get back to you* diligence. Digital robo-advisors that are available to the customer (member or client) ahead of the session would help in focusing the conversation and driving to better and faster outcomes.

DIGITAL IMPACT ON BRICK-AND-MORTAR

In-person interaction preferences for financial transactions will consequently shift. People are growing used to trusting digital face-to-face interactions and intelligent self-service tools. And many will favor the convenience of conducting business from the comfort of their home or office, as well as on-the-go.

Many locations around the world are facing continual challenges regarding personal safety as well as the transportation time and cost that are involved in a branch visit. Hence, the ability to carry out financial transactions remotely will be welcomed by all involved. New digital ways of doing business remotely will also transform the role of the financial brick-and-mortar points of service.

The implementation of self-service technology in digitally intensive branches and financial centers will free branch staff to spend more time with customers, clients, and members while bringing the benefits of more efficient transaction processing. Branches will be tightly integrated with other delivery channels, giving consumers the channel choice that best meets their needs.

> The shift in focus from bricks-to-clicks reflects an industry obsession with providing the best experience possible. And questions abound among financial institutions about the efficacy of their respective branch networks. Branch numbers and sizes will shrink (with potentially substantial savings in real estate costs) as branches continue to be less transaction-oriented and more focused on service and product fulfilment.
>
> Taking a 2030 perspective, financial services will be truly digitized: consumers and businesses will conduct the vast majority of their transactions and interactions through an unprecedented range of access points, and the number of

physical branches will have reduced significantly - perhaps by as much as 30 percent from today's levels (Sievewright, Branch Banking in a Digital World, 2018).

In many ways, branches of the future will show a blend of digital and physical experiences. And consumers will also develop a digital presence of their own. As digital interactions take hold everywhere, the identity of individuals will be expressed not only in their personal information or biometric parameters but also in their digital behaviors and profile.

The nature of what we refer to today as our social media presence will change. In the uber-connected world of 2030, each of us will have a personalized digital presence or capability (which goes well beyond today's Facebook, Twitter, or Instagram!) that becomes the hub of how we manage our lives, including our financial services relationships.

The momentous societal shifts are being driven—to a very large extent—by advances in technology. Way beyond what we have today, by 2030, we will have highly advanced ways to share information, procure products and services and manage our daily routines, including broad-scale use of artificial intelligence (Sievewright, Finding the Future - The World in 2030, 2017).

THE DIGITAL EXPERIENCE BRANCH

As the number of physical branches keeps dwindling and relying more on digital services, how will futuristic branches look like after 2030? What will digital-savvy consumers appreciate the most in a branch? Anything but the traditional and most unwelcoming branch layout, where tellers hide behind a (protective) physical barrier of metal bars or bullet-proof glass is the most likely answer. The value proposition of the branch will evolve from being a secure place to transact with cash or valuables to a well-equipped site that crystalizes the digital experience of the client, customer, or member.

Many people will enjoy intelligent digital technologies at their homes of the future. Advances in artificial intelligence and robotics will result in affordable service gadgets. For instance, autonomous appliances in the shape of roaming robots that fulfill a variety of chores such as vacuum cleaning, mowing the lawn, babysitting, brewing coffee, and providing personalized butler services. As homes feature advanced technologies, why would anybody put up with an inferior level of digital equipment and services when visiting a branch?

For future branches, the first challenge will be to attract a then-dominant majority of digital-savvy individuals. Fortunately, digital technologies will come to the rescue and will play a pivotal role in luring people to the branches. For passers-by, a visible display of the latest technology gimmicks combined with glaring and inviting signage may do the trick.

Most impactfully, a personalized, relevant, and timely invitation will pop up on smartphones or wearable devices. A basic one: come on in! You were waiting for money markets to move; shall we discuss how today's rates work in your favor?

In such a scenario, financial institutions would have obtained the required opt-in permissions to allay any privacy constraints. They would have garnered comprehensive records of the individual's interactions through all channels, whether attended or unattended, or whether these took place with the institution or a third-party provider, financial or non-financial. And they would have applied sophisticated personalization algorithms to factor the individual's wants and needs, interaction preferences, schedule, whereabouts, and financial situation.

Stepping into the digital branch, visitors will feel at home. Live television screens and digital displays have already become an expected feature at branches, so what else will be there?

Several institutions have been successfully experimenting with hybrid branch spaces that combine coffee bars, comfortable sitting spaces with tables and other areas seen in retail stores. To serve upscale clients, many banks have already architected a private atmosphere with fine furniture and plush sofas. What will make branches function more like a home?

Many branches have been featuring a prominent greeter desk, equipped with system access to provide guidance and attend simple queries directly. Yes, digital branches will still build on the warmth, charm, and empathy of trusted human touch displayed by people-minded greeters. Predictive analytics, presence sensors, and cognitive analysis of the visitor will instantly augment their understanding of the context and personalized best actions. New branch layout concepts will evolve the greeter stations into more home-like reception areas. And what else?

Figure 8 – A 5-star digital greeter

A spacious, multifunction entry area will welcome visitors. Depending on the location and space, this entry area may blend selected decor and features that are commonly found in residential great rooms, family rooms, and coffee bars. It would allow visitors to visualize other home-like branch sectors. For instance, an open view to adjacent areas acting like living rooms or playrooms may be incorporated.

Visitors may also readily find digital guidance through interactive displays, roaming robots, and smartphone apps. Much like technology stores, showcasing the latest technology fad will entice visitors to try them out.

Visitors would have the freedom to choose their preferred mode of interaction, attended or digital, and navigate seamlessly across the available channels. Financial institutions will find it advantageous to pivot on their own branded, intelligent app.

Besides providing personalized guidance into digital branches, this branded app would also serve as a portal to a wide range of financial and lifestyle services. As visitors identify themselves and start articulating their needs or possible interests, they will be ushered into the appropriate branch sector.

For example, visitors will want to explore and apply for a personalized home loan. In such a scenario, visitors would be invited to sit comfortably in a home-like area combining living-room and library settings. The personalized app would allow them to simulate financing alternatives projected on a digital wall and find out what class of property they could reach within their acquisition power.

Advanced digital capabilities would provide virtual reality headsets that teleport visitors to a digital twin image of the actual property. Similar digital experiences would also cater to financing vacation plans, college education, and automobiles.

For many, the closing step in such a productive branch journey would culminate at a financial advisor position. In what may resemble a homely, integrated kitchen and dining room setting, advisors would prepare the optimal gourmet concoction of financial (and lifestyle) offerings to delight the visitor and close the deal. Many transaction parameters would have already been pre-selected and vetted.

And the deal table would include several technology features that are already found in digital boardrooms. Coffee, drinks, and treats would sweeten the deal. Advisors may readily share the deal on-the-spot. Collaborative videoconferences will pull in available product specialists, supervisors, and third parties. Digital documentation and interconnection with the ecosystem of supporting systems will make it frictionless. As depicted in *Exhibit 9*, the attended and digital journey through the digital branch would lead visitors to enjoy a highly personalized, most productive, and homely experience.

Visitor journey through the digital experience branch

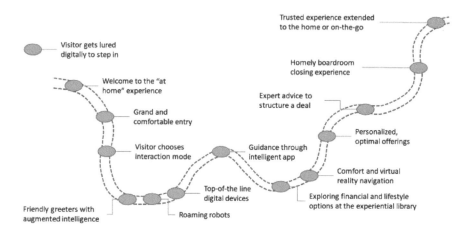

Exhibit 9 – Visitor journey through the digital experience branch

THE UBIQUITOUS DIGITAL BRANCH

As financial institutions pivot on branded intelligent apps to help with the customer journey at the digital experience branch, they may overcome the physical limitations of brick-and-mortar. Institutions would be able to extend the branch anytime to wherever the customer, client, or member may happen to be. Riding on the intimate and experiential knowledge gained during the branch visit, the interaction could continue digitally at their car, home, or place of business. Videoconferencing and voice-activated chatbots would supplement the multifaceted capabilities of the intelligent app.

Trust is a defining factor when establishing a relationship with a financial institution. For most individuals, the in-person experience will be decisive and branches will play a pivotal role. Here, direct rapport with branch personnel fed by face-to-face interactions, proper behavioral traits, as well as verbal and non-verbal cues, will nurture trust.

Mobile digital videoconferencing may build up the face-to-face interactions and reaffirm the trusted relationship with the institution. Establishing personal connections through social media would also contribute to the continuity of the branch experience.

Many institutions wonder whether they should support a larger or smaller branch network. However, the experiential success of a branch will hinge on its human and digital intensity. The experience will be most powerful when deploying intelligent apps and advanced technologies to augment the behavioral traits and situational knowledge of branch personnel. And the creatively crafted, home-like attributes of the digital experience branch will transcend the brick-and-mortar walls and continue in a timely manner, most comfortably and ubiquitously, at home or on-the-go.

In his letter to shareholders of March 3, 2020, Brian Moynihan, the chairman and CEO of Bank of America, highlighted their digital progress:

> The investment in our financial centers and ATMs goes beyond modernizing existing centers and building new ones. It connects all our client services and experiences and creates the opportunity to build on existing relationships and attract new ones. As our clients' needs and expectations evolve, the financial center client experience and design has to evolve with them . . . . Our AI-driven digital assistant, Erica®, was

launched in 2018, and we topped 10 million users last year...
Another example is our Aira service—a new technology to
help blind and low-vision clients gain better access to our
financial centers and ATMs. Digital channels generated 29
percent of overall sales, with 34 percent of mortgages and 56
percent of auto loans now originating in our mobile app or
online banking site (Bank of America, 2020).

Along similar lines in his letter to shareholders of Citigroup,
Michael L. Corbat, chief executive officer, reflected on the relevance
of investing in new digital experiences: "We are targeting a significant
opportunity to redefine scale, not according to the traditional
metrics of assets and footprint but with digitally driven experiences
(Citigroup, 2020)."

ENRICHING THE CUSTOMER (MEMBER) EXPERIENCE

As a result of strategic work with several credit unions in
developing a digital strategy the following key result areas and
baseline questions provide a focused foundation for transformation
projects (Sievewright, Digital Transaction Management and
Transformation, 2019):

Member Experience:
- In your business or product area, what meaningful
  improvements could be made to enhance the member
  experience?
- Have you identified areas where you can make it easier for
  members to do business with the credit union?
- What obstacles exist to implementing improvements in
  member service, product delivery, and distribution?

Member Engagement:

• For your business or product area, how could your credit union grow/deepen the relationships it has with its members?

• Using digital tools, how could your credit union more effectively communicate with, engage with, and market to, its members?

Empowered Members and Staff:

• In what ways could your credit union provide members with more direct control over (and access to) their financial relationships?

• What digital tools or additional data could your credit union staff use to allow them to be even more effective in doing their jobs?

Efficiency and Effectiveness:

• What inefficiencies or obstacles exist within your credit union's current operating processes and/or the technologies that support them?

• Using digital tools, how could your credit union improve the overall effectiveness of its business and/or individual product areas?

DIGITAL VILLAGES

Digital technologies are transforming the canvas of urban life. Various intelligent devices, such as Amazon's Alexa, now available on more than 100 million devices (Amazon, 2020), are invading people's homes. Cars have digital sensors to track the vehicle's performance, and the dashboards connect to apps and services that are available through the driver's smartphone.

Most significantly, digital devices and sensors in offices and factories are generating a wealth of data continually. Public utilities, such as electricity grids or transport services, increasingly depend on digital technologies to optimize their efficiency in real time. How will the massive flow of digital information pouring from billions of these sources affect everyday life?

Beyond the intrinsic benefits that individuals and enterprises may derive from the devices and related services, municipalities are developing smart urban services. Of course, the administration of any city, town, or village may capitalize on rich and timely information. Furthermore, the emerging digital infrastructure coupled with the pervasive interconnectivity of public and private activities, is giving rise to a new breed of urban digital services. Technology innovators are calling them *smart cities*.

Digital life has already felt the impact of real-time social media activity, particularly the capture of live scenes on Facebook and Twitter. As highlighted in *Exhibit 10* (Statista, 2020), millions of individuals use social media globally. And people may broadcast their perceptions as they occur. Some multimedia content may go viral.

For instance, live video of noteworthy events, such as a popular music concert, odd behaviors in public venues, and even crime scenes are broadcast. The impact transcends the purposes of newscasters or social curiosity and may reshape the actual behaviors of the people involved.

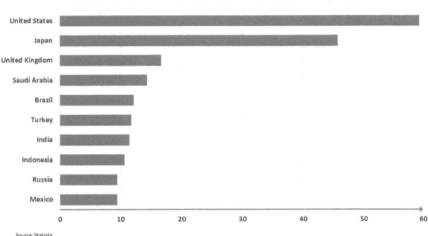

Exhibit 10 – Millions of Twitter users (January 2020)

Live experiences may go beyond what human senses may capture directly. The use of smartphones to share and add instant comments about an event would augment the thrill to the bearer. Subsequent interactions through social media may rapidly multiply the individual experience and convert it into collective digital value. In summary, live digital media will add new experiential dimensions.

Innovative real-time digital services for the everyday city life will find many practical use cases. A few examples of transformational applications would include mobile parking, dynamic signage, transport fleet and traffic optimization, government and marketplace transactions, grid communications, supply chain optimization, and digital twins of buildings, public sites, and stations. Municipalities may also offer digital services for public health, safety and security, and citizen engagement. How will this interconnected urban digital life affect financial institutions?

For starters, most of the money in circulation will be digital. Then, the exchange or digital value will become a component in virtually every urban interaction. For example, the pervasiveness of personal and intelligent IoT devices will intertwine digital services with the physical movement of goods and people.

Hence the emergence of creative combinations of digital currencies embedded in these services. In this context, financial institutions will face a strategic crossroad: to offer services proactively in partnership with the digital village ecosystem, or to be relegated to a back-office role. And business models to bolster the digital urban experience will thrive on a new source of revenue: the wealth of digital data.

WILL COVID-19 LEAD TO DIGITAL STADIUMS?

The tragic COVID-19 pandemic served as wake-up call to the entire world that physical proximity could spread the disease rapidly and exponentially, thus turning this ultra-contagious infection into a fatal liability. A first line of defense against such an aggressive and contagious virus hinged on the ability of the population to observe social distancing safeguards and slow down the spread. What will happen to highly popular massive sports events, concerts, and rallies that gather tens of thousands of spectators as a compactly packed crowd?

Restricting the number of people sitting or standing next to each other represents a tactical preventative move. However, such limitations would be unsustainable in the long run since they would undermine the collective and personal experience and the economic viability of the infrastructure.

A similar logic would behoove the financial services branches, particularly in those locations that get significant foot traffic. It would be quite awkward to find customers willing to line up outside a branch in inclement weather due to strict limitations in the number of people allowed inside at any time.

Financial institutions could find some inspiration from sports events. For example, football (soccer) is one of the most popular sports globally, with over two billion people watching a world-cup final. Of course, it would be unthinkable to squeeze that many people into a stadium.

Besides, hot-ticket events usually have much higher demand than what the venue may accommodate. In European football, several franchises are learning how to capitalize on the global demand from millions of fans into fantastic commercial opportunities.

Advanced digital technologies will provide a way to attend such massive demand at scale and discover innovative ways to monetize it. For instance, in a digital *freemium* model, sports franchises may stream most games for free and charge a fee for those that are in high demand.

Moreover, such digital relationships reach out to about a thousand times more people than could possibly fit a physical stadium. Coupled with savvy marketing, a franchise may sell personalized digital services for individual subscribers to access, replay, and track the great moves, scores, and stories of their favorite stars.

In the US, the National Basketball Association (NBA) announced an alliance with Microsoft that will transform the way fans experience the games (Microsoft Corporation, 2020). A direct-to-consumer cloud platform will reimagine how fans engage with the NBA from their digital devices. The NBA will localize the digital experiences for its global base of 1.8 billion social media followers.

Sport teams will tap a technology known as *digital twins* to mimic the in-stadium experience. Digital twins reproduce a physical facility, in excruciating detail, as an intelligent three dimensional visualization that may incorporate virtual reality effects. This technology will allow fans to experience, augment, and relive within a virtual stadium the energy and enthusiasm of the actual physical event.

By a similar token and building on the construct of a digital experience branch, financial institutions will find many opportunities to extend the physical experience to the virtual world. Not only will secure videoconferencing and mixed reality technologies provide the flexibility to keep their services operational during physical restrictions at branches, but they will open new revenue sources and creative avenues to sustain client, customer, or member relationships.

MASSIVE DIGITAL LENDING

Along with the harsh experience of COVID-19, what will happen with hundreds of thousands of small businesses that suffer a prolonged slowdown or stoppage? As the financial system gests called (and funded) to rescue them, emergency lending will still carry some level of credit risk.

For many financial institutions, the big challenge is how to originate, analyze, approve, and operationalize thousands of new credit facilities in a short period of time. Oftentimes, legacy core systems, credit administration operations, and approval policies get in the way of responding fast enough to such challenging demand. Conversely, nimble fintech digital lending schema may rise better to the challenge.

As lending represents a core financial services competency, it is high time that institutions took to heart transformative modernization strategies. Besides significantly improving their readiness for an unexpected surge in demand, a digital and thorough revamp of the commercial credit process will bring immediate benefits to the institution and their small business customers. Central to such a modernization approach, the cornerstone will be an ability to orchestrate digital, collaborative workflows. To swing into full automation and manage risk adequately, financial institutions may tap predictive analytics and artificial intelligence tools, such as chatbots and cognitive services.

LEVERAGING THE RICH WORLD OF DIGITAL DATA

The digital village will enable an intimate understanding of the whereabouts and activities of every individual, enterprise, government agency, public utility, and infrastructure component. And the ability to turn such live information into intelligent offerings and on-the-spot services that bring a swift, optimal, and efficient experience will unlock new value opportunities.

Financial institutions will then need to rethink their role above and beyond a mere tactical quest to partake in digital payments. They will also need to extend the role of their intelligent, digitally enabled branches and remote videoconferencing channels beyond traditional conversations. Instead of focusing almost exclusively on financial products and services, institutions will need to ride on the new realities of the digital village and play a more relevant role in the emerging lifestyles of their customers, clients, or members.

Indeed, playing a forefront role in the digital value exchange will allow institutions to capture the most precious digital resource: rich personal data. Social media providers have already realized such strategic value: "Libra might be best seen not as a financial newcomer, but as a critical enabler for Facebook to acquire a new source of personal data" (Valerie Khan, 2019).

Financial institutions are gaining increasingly rich transaction insights garnered at their own branches and through a continuing development and penetration of intelligent digital channels. Given the privacy and secrecy restrictions in the heavily regulated financial industry, how will institutions find a competitive edge?

Most institutions will first need to visualize the big digital picture and develop new strengths as digital marketeers, or at least establish strategic alliances with leading players in this field. And they will need to learn how to lure individuals into lifestyle experiences, getting them to opt-in eagerly and share a succulent chunk of their personal information, habits, and preferences.

In a nutshell: financial institutions will need to break out from the confines of the walls of their branches and offices, see beyond their traditional role, seize the value of live data, and develop a relevant presence in the daily life of the digital village.

REFERENCES

Amazon. (2020). *Amazon Alexa*. Retrieved from Amazon: https://developer.amazon.com/en-US/alexa

Bank of America. (2020, March). *2019 Annual Report*. Retrieved from Investor Relations: http://investor.bankofamerica.com/static-files/898007fd-033d-4f32-8470-c1f316c73b24

Citigroup. (2020, April). *2019 Annual Report*. Retrieved from Investor Relations: https://www.citigroup.com/citi/investor/quarterly/2020/ar19_en.pdf?ieNocache=548

Microsoft Corporation. (2020). *Smart Cities*. Retrieved from Microsoft Industry: https://www.microsoft.com/en-us/industry/government/smart-cities

Microsoft Corporation. (2020, April 16). *Stories*. Retrieved from Microsoft News Center: https://news.microsoft.com/2020/04/16/nba-announces-new-multiyear-partnership-with-microsoft-to-redefine-and-personalize-the-fan-experience/

Sievewright, M. (2017, November). *Finding the Future - The World in 2030*. Retrieved from Perspectives: https://sievewright-andassociates.com/

Sievewright, M. (2018, August). *Branch Banking in a Digital World.* Retrieved from Perspectives Report: https://sievewrightandassociates.com/

Sievewright, M. (2019). *Digital Transaction Management and Transformation.* Sievewright & Associates.

Statista. (2020, January). *Internet - Social Media & User-Generated Content.* Retrieved from statista: https://www.statista.com/statistics/242606/number-of-active-twitter-users-in-selected-countries/

Valerie Khan, G. G. (2019, August). *Libra: Is it Really about Money?* Retrieved from Cornell University: https://arxiv.org/abs/1908.07474v1

5.
NEW ANALYTICS WITH ARTIFICIAL INTELLIGENCE

ANCESTORS OF DIGITAL INTELLIGENCE

TO UNDERSTAND THE DIGITAL FUTURE, it is important to learn from past developments in analytics and computing in general. In prehistoric times, humans piled up pebbles as elementary counters. As early as 2700 BC the abacus, a counting frame, appeared in ancient Mesopotamia and China and persisted through modern times as an education tool.

The Latin word for pebble is "calculus," which gave rise to the modern word calculator. As in ancient Rome, the word calculator "has been used since the sixteenth century to refer to someone who calculates, or who is skilled in arithmetical procedures, or by extension, who is skilled in planning and scheming" (Ifrah, 2001). Ancient civilizations were keen on counting things and monetary instruments. Only in the seventeenth century did astronomers and tax collectors feel the urge for faster calculations.

Among several pioneering designs toward a mechanical calculator, the German astronomer Wilhelm Schickard wrote a letter in 1623 describing his construction of "a machine which, immediately and automatically, adds, subtracts, multiplies, and divides" (Marguin, 1994).

However, the mechanical calculator is credited to Blaise Pascal, the famous French mathematician and philosopher. Pascal had developed several calculating machine prototypes. In 1645, he dedicated his *Pascaline*, the first one with a carrying mechanism, to the chancellor of France (Pascal, 1645). Mechanical calculators helped with a faster way to do simple arithmetical operations manually but lacked any intelligence.

In 1821, Charles Babbage started building a first version of his *difference engine*, a more complex mechanical calculator of decimal digits. As the physical construction turned out to be too heavy and onerous, the project was halted.

Then Babbage shifted gears to design a more generic and capable machine, introduced in 1834 and presently known as the analytical engine, which stands out as the first programmable computer concept (Swade, n.d.). But mechanical computers were still slow, and extremely burdensome to build at scale, given the weight of so many metallic gears and levers.

The widely recognized precursor of digital computers and artificial intelligence stems from the works of Alan Turing. In 1937, Turing conceived a theoretical computing machine with infinite capacity that could be implemented as unlimited variations in practical forms of universal computers (Turing, On Computable Numbers, with an Application to the Entscheidungsproblem, 1937).

Such an abstract Turing machine would solve a much broader range of problems than mechanical computers but still at limited speeds. Given such infinite processing capacity and theoretical flexibility to tackle many a challenge, Turing machines were said to reason intelligently. But would such machines reach parity or surpass human abilities?

At the beginning of his article *Computing Machinery and Intelligence*, Turing proposed the question, "Can machines think?" He reframed this challenge in the form of an experiment, which is known as the Turing Test. This experiment stems from a guessing game known as the *imitation game* (Turing, Computing Machinery and Intelligence, 1950).

In the Turing Test, an interrogator seeks to determine which of two respondents, one human and another a computer, is indeed a computer. Turing's challenge was "whether there are imaginable computers that would do well" in this test. Notwithstanding this foundational teaser for artificial intelligence, it would take a couple of decades for digital computers to feature enough capacity and speed to start processing relatively complex challenges.

In 1965, a creative team of professors, associates, and students at Stanford University launched the Dendral Project in artificial intelligence. This project introduced one of the first large-scale expert systems, which intended to reproduce human knowledge and decision making. The concept entailed using detailed, task-specific knowledge about a problem domain as a source of heuristics, to seek generality through automating the acquisition of such knowledge (Feigenbaum, 1993).

A salient feature was to separate the knowledge base about a specific domain, represented as rules learned from human experts, from the computer code to interpret such knowledge. A decade later, Marvin Minsky published a more advanced framework around the human representation of knowledge.

Figure 9 – Analytics and human knowledge

Minsky introduced the concept of *frames* (Minsky, 1974), which are data structures with schemas and links. Minsky's frames postulate how human memory represents stereotyped situations and adapts them to interpret reality.

ANALYTICS VERSUS DIGITAL POTENTIAL

Over the past four decades, advances in computing power, data analytics, and artificial intelligence have turned the promise of digital machine concepts into astounding realities. Artificial intelligence developments have accelerated significantly in the last decade and this science is becoming the leading field in digital innovation. Furthermore, artificial intelligence tools are becoming broadly available to software developers and intelligent applications are beginning to permeate our daily lives.

As science meets computing capacity and digital ingenuity, artificial intelligence serves as a robust and plausible foundation to augment human intelligence. A most telling development is the emerging infusion of artificial intelligence into analytics.

For example, practical applications of advanced analytics are integrating speech recognition and translation (Amershi, 2019) with design recommendations and guidelines to influence better, more human-centric systems that infuse artificial intelligence. It is important to note that artificial intelligence entails several advanced computing capabilities, such as:

Figure 10 – Artificial intelligence in financial services

- Machine learning: instant computing capability to analyze extensive and seemingly disparate sets of data and perform effective classification, anomaly detection, pattern recognition, and projections. New algorithms known as extreme classification serve as an example of what advanced analytics can accomplish.

  Extreme classification algorithms may search through 100 million multi-label input records in a matter of milliseconds (Microsoft Research, 2019). Effective machine learning models ride on the wisdom of multiple libraries of data science algorithms and converge dependably to consistent analyses. These advanced analytics are capable of detecting anomalies or patterns which may escape human detection.

- Cognitive services: more adaptive and sophisticated computing frameworks that pivot on deep learning processing structures also known as neural networks. When properly configured and trained for the task at hand, cognitive services may perform human-like functions such as computer vision and speech translation (Natural Language Understanding).

  Practical implementations of cognitive services include universal language translators that can process text or voice input in real-time. The mobile app Seeing AI provides a similar example, as it is aimed at assisting individuals with visual disabilities. This intelligent app can read out what the device sees, powered by real-time image and video captioning, face recognition, and object detection capabilities.

- Chatbots: building on machine learning and cognitive services functions, conversational chatbots are the quintessential implementation of Turing's imitation game. Instead of seeking to trick an interrogator into believing that they are interacting with a human being, chatbots answer freewheeling questions and assist with relatively simple tasks. Should the interaction transcend the chatbot's knowledge or programmed capabilities then the customer conversation, together with its context, gets handed over seamlessly to the proper human agent.

  Chatbots may accumulate significant domain knowledge through many thousands, or even millions, of real-life interactions. Advanced conversational AI features may enable contextual learning and language and personality understanding. Practical applications include an emerging breed of intelligent personal agents such as Amazon's Alexa, Microsoft's Cortana, or Google's Siri. Future generations of super chatbots will take the stage in our lives as digital companions at home, in the car, at work, and virtually everywhere.

Common features of artificial intelligence models are that they need to be trained and tested with representative samples of data and learn about the corresponding outcomes. To be effective over time, these models should have the ability to learn from real-life experience or otherwise be retrained.

Given the higher speed and hyperscale capacity and speed of cloud computing, sophisticated analytics and artificial intelligence models can run in quasi real-time. Therefore, thanks to cloud computing, it is increasingly easier to resolve complex problems instantly.

These life-changing developments are creating a chasm between the traditional domain of analytics, and the many emerging applications of artificial intelligence. Traditional analytics are oftentimes referred to as a look into the rearview mirror, since they focus on past data, events, and insights. Most of the digital data that gets fed into analytic engines is structured, meaning specific text and numeric fields.

In contrast, artificial intelligence brings advanced capabilities to interpret both structured and unstructured data (such as speech, images, and video) that are unlocking a very promising potential. The schematic in *Exhibit 11* depicts the chasm between past and future potential. It also highlights four transformative applications of artificial intelligence in the analytics world.

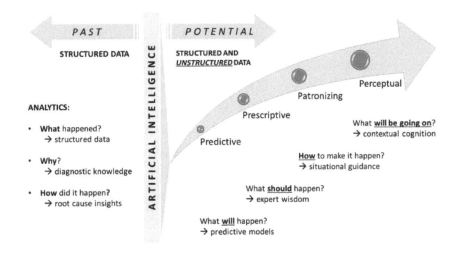

Exhibit 11 – Analytics, Artificial Intelligence, and Cognitive Services

Namely, these transformative dimensions are:

- **Predictive analytics**: given multiple data series and variables, machine learning models can make accurate projections of future values. Whereas the human mind tends to attribute an absolute truth of such predictions, these are just probability values. For example, a very strong prediction may have a 95 percent probability of occurrence, but it also means that the opposite outcome may happen 5 percent of the time. Still these are reasonably good predictions about what will most probably happen.

- **Prescriptive analytics**: By combining the power of machine learning, the adaptability of deep learning, the wisdom of expert systems, and the empirical simulations of game theory, these more advanced models may evaluate a given situation against complex scenarios. The outcome consists in recommended, practical actions or values that should optimize a set of variables against possible scenarios.

Practical implementations would be maximizing the yields of investment portfolios against the expected market conditions.

- **Patronizing guidance**: Getting into the artificial intelligence engines underpinning real-life robots, the prescriptions may be enriched by continual feedback from multiple sensors or other live data input or streams. Logic structures and algorithms can represent the real world through complex arrays of situational states, transition rules, heuristics, and learned strategies. These engines provide situational guidance on strategies and actions to attain a desired outcome. A practical, albeit still simple example, would be an artificial intelligence model to empower an average chess player to beat any grand master.

- **Perceptual cognition**: A higher level of sophisticated models, sensors, and algorithms will mimic humans with a surprisingly capable set of digital senses. Building on the current attainments in speech and video processing, all human senses will be in scope. Equipped with superior experimentation, self-evolution, and accumulated learning, such a high level of digital cognition can be perfectly aware of the surrounding context. It will also be capable of sensing live situations and predict, in real-time, what will be going on and act proactively. Suffice it to say that service robots will belong in this category.

These dimensions offer a glimpse into the real potential of artificial intelligence. Getting there however, will take a transformative design-thinking mindset. People tend to draw general conclusions about what digital computers can or cannot do based on the computers that have been seen in operation.

Still lacking a complete understanding of our own human nature, engineers unwittingly create intelligent computer programs to mimic their own semblance and surroundings. Hence, organizations will experience a polarizing effect. On one side are skeptics that cannot visualize the digital potential beyond what is already available in existing automated solutions. On the other hand are enthusiasts who readily grasp and embrace transformative innovations based on early prototypes or breakthroughs.

Cognitive services will continue to attain, and even surpass, human parity. Artificial intelligence algorithms are designed to learn and improve their own capabilities. "Processes fulfilling these roles of replication, variation and selection can be implemented in a computer, resulting in an evolutionary algorithm. Such learning can be simulated by randomly perturbing elements within a given data structure. So well-intentioned quantitative measures are often maximized in counter-intuitive ways" (Lehman, 2018). This digital evolution can learn to recognize and exploit subtle patterns that may come up during the evolutionary learning simulation process.

With all these digital advances, what will be the impact on our daily lives? Artificial intelligence will affect in different ways the many diverse human personalities, psyches, and attitudes toward work and study. A most interesting reflection comes from a 2030 vision from Stanford University:

> Because AI systems perform work that previously required human labor, they have the effect of lowering the cost of many goods and services, effectively making everyone richer... As labor becomes a less important factor in production as compared to owning intellectual capital, a majority of citizens may find the value of their labor insufficient to pay for a socially acceptable standard of living... The enthusiasm with which humans have responded to AI-driven entertainment has been surprising and led to concerns that it reduces interpersonal interaction among human beings. Few predicted that people would spend hours on end interacting with a display. Children often appear to be genuinely happier playing at home on

their devices rather than outside with their friends. Artificial intelligence will increasingly enable entertainment that is more interactive, personalized, and engaging Artificial Intelligence and Life in 2030 (Stanford University, 2016).

DATA-DRIVEN DIGITAL DECISION MAKING

Most company executives favor some sort of data-driven decisions. As executives are surrounded by a multitude of digital insights and expert opinions, they strive to arrive at sound decisions in a timely fashion. The ability to turn actionable insights into effective decisions would ultimately reside in the eyes of the beholder.

The accuracy and completeness of digital calculations or the insightfulness coming from artificial intelligence algorithms are still bound to the nuances of human perception and interpretation. For example, a predominantly analytical personality would tend to trust calculations, insights, and rationale and act upon them. On the other hand, a strongly intuitive personality would need to interpret the results in further context before arriving at a conclusion.

Therefore, the way to present and help visualize digital analytics or artificial intelligence insights should mind the different personalities or the decision makers. A widely used tool for gauging personalities is the Myers-Briggs Type Indicator® (The Myers & Briggs Foundation, n.d.) that categorizes individual perception based on personal interaction styles and preferences. This indicator describes sixteen distinctive personality types that stem from the possible combinations of individual preferences and traits, namely:

- Extraversion (E) or Introversion (I): whether a person focuses on the external or inner world.
- Sensing (S) or Intuition (N): whether the focus is on basic

information, or its own interpretation.

- Thinking (T) or Feeling (F): whether a person starts decisions using logic, or people and circumstances.
- Judging (J) or Perceiving (P): whether to decide on known structures or stay open to new information.

Even when dealing with seemingly straightforward financial analytics, the human factor will come into play. For example, a credit officer may overcome an analytical (sensing) inclination and heed a compelling set of special circumstances to approve an otherwise risky loan. And a predominantly intuitive trader may rely on his or her experience and feel of the capital markets to override quantitative insights or risk indicators.

Advanced analytics systems should go above and beyond digital computations. Successful systems will articulate a thorough explanation underpinning the analytic insights, allow for flexible and friendly visualization styles, and help navigate the rationale supporting the recommended actions. Ultimately, the outcomes will depend on how people use their common sense, which still represents a distinctive advantage of humans over digital computers.

HUMAN DECISIONS AND DIGITAL LOGIC

To get the most value out of their common sense, humans face several challenges and constraints. For example, the willingness to acknowledge and pass judgment based on the facts and underlying rationale. Which means the honesty to overcome any form of personal bias. Subjective bias may cause people to set aside proper facts or insights and ignore or distort truthful data sources. And complicate or even derail the conclusions by referencing unreliable data sources or unsubstantiated insights.

As the increasing velocity of digital information becomes overwhelming, common sense is put to the test. Some personality types would comfortably act on digital information alone. And others would vacillate for too long even when facing a most compelling and comprehensive set of insights and recommendations.

Even the simpler formulations may be subject to a human error of interpretation. Typical issues include a lack of attention to basic calculation and algebraic details, as well as incongruent use of logic. A common pitfall stems from stubbornly carrying over their acquired trust on false hypotheses.

In logic, if the antecedent argument is false, then the implication would hold true regardless of the intended consequent. A false antecedent causes the whole implication to hold true, as reflected in the logic formula: NOT (antecedent) OR (consequent). When people reach implied conclusions that are assumed to be true, but were based on false antecedents, then the conclusion may turn out to be factually irrelevant.

And people may have limitations. Understanding projections that track to counterintuitive exponential scales, multiple dimensions, or massively concurrent events, may often escape the grasp of the typical human reasoning. Digital technologies keep propelling advances in sciences such as quantum mechanics, nuclear physics, astrophysics, and brain neurology.

However, people may oftentimes seek to map still unexplained phenomena against their mundane frames of reference, even when such theories prove to be inadequate. Could digital conclusions then be more truthful than people?

Given the variations in personal interpretation, the incidence of procedural errors, biased analyses, human limitations, and scientific uncertainties, it seems wise that decisions include a diversity of thought. A wisdom of diversity of opinion is rooted deeply in many cultures and was thoughtfully coined in classical drama plays. A quote in ancient Latin reads: "Audiatur et altera pars" (the other side shall also be heard). It appeared in the plays of Aeschylus (525–456 BC), an ancient Greek tragedian author, and Seneca (4 BC–AD 65), a Roman statesperson, philosopher, and dramatist.

In *Eumenides* (Johnston, 2002), the last play of a trilogy fiction by Aeschylus that narrated a vengeful succession of family murders, the accused Orestes is put to trial. After a blast from "fury" plaintiffs, the Queen presiding the trial opens to an offsetting defense that prompts Orestes' acquittal.

Indeed, such right to confront the evidence is considered as a fundamental principle of justice in most legal systems. By analogy, in today's digital world, sensible subject matter experts and seasoned data science professionals should also allow for divergent artificial intelligence insights. In an increasingly complex and intertwined global economy and capital markets, people need digital technology and smart collaboration to sustain the quality and timeliness of business decisions.

Reaffirming the ancient wisdom to let others be heard, it is worth noting some everyday work principles articulated by Ray Dalio, an influential investor, leading hedge fund founder, and philanthropist. For example, Ray's reflections on the importance of other ideas: "Inexperienced people can have great ideas too, sometimes *far better* ones than more experienced people" (Principle 5.2 E).

An open-minded stance that captures diverse ideas, both from people and artificial intelligence output, should contribute to the quality of decisions. Would such improvement in decision quality justify the extra time that it may take?

First and foremost, decision makers should better understand the rationale behind any such constructive idea or conclusion. Ray Dalio has also quipped: "Don't pay as much attention to people's conclusions as to the reasoning that led them to their conclusions" (Principle 5.2 D). In the digital world, advanced artificial intelligence algorithms are now capable of explaining in a transparent manner the factors and path that led a given conclusion. Notwithstanding an abundance of transparency, what happens then when people struggle to agree on difficult decisions?

When open to persuasive insights, facts, rationales, and recommendations, both in-person and videoconference discussions may get stalled in protracted debate. Ray Dalio also reflects on this issue: "Know when to stop debating and move on to agreeing on what should be done. I have seen people who agree on the major issues waste hours arguing over details. It's more important to do big things well than to do the small things perfectly" (Principle 5.5A).

In today's fast-paced digital world, this fundamental principle is becoming more crucial. Mired in the search for the absolute, risk-free truth and unanimous consensus, executive decisions may come too late to be effective or even relevant. Diversity of thought, to include intelligent digital input, actionable conclusions, and constructive agreement should lead to better and faster decisions.

DECISIONS IN A DIGITAL WORLD

Thwarting a diligent, holistic, and pragmatic decision approach, continual waves of rapidly flowing digital messages, images, and video-clips may shake some people. And inherent bias and preconceived ideas may trigger people to react instantly to specific snippets of information that stand out amid this digital tsunami.

Instead of reflecting on the merit of first impressions and their sources, rushing to conclusions seems to bode naturally with today's digital world. And people may deliberately or unwittingly accept, and react to, partial digital information instantly and without giving it further thought.

Viral rushes to action may bring damaging consequences. On one extreme, orchestrated cyberattacks and disinformation campaigns may result in collective digital brainwashing to sway people's opinion toward a prejudiced direction.

Conversely, detecting and filtering out apparent attempts that push unacceptable bias through digital media may create intrinsic and escalating censorship that would clash with an utmost diverse and freewheeling digital world. Much in the same way that digital decisions still benefit from a diversity of thought, global and pervasive digital media needs to adhere to moral principles and values.

The challenge of information ethics gets compounded as any given community, or even a nation, may lag the level of diversity that prevails in today's global digital world. The dangers may be illustrated by some highly polarized examples. The dystopian novel *1984* by English writer George Orwell and published in 1949 pictures a futuristic state where people "have become victims of perpetual war, omnipresent government surveillance and propaganda" (Murphy, 1996).

As organizations and cyber-states are caught orchestrating blatant information hacks, Orwell's fiction seems to be turning into reality. *Alphaville* (Godard, 1965), a somewhat related dystopian film, portrays a controlling government that issues frequent new versions of an official dictionary that suppresses forbidden words. As digital diversity and hyper-personalization may stoke new cultural sensitivities, an emerging mode of reaction would resort to vehemently shun words that were deemed to convey an offensive connotation.

Another polarized example that is grounded in present realities: a continual fixation on instant messages and attached media and commentary, news clips, and online activity may give rise to cyber-dependent personalities. In such pathology, individuals may rely more on digital (and fleeting) interactions than direct in-person deeds and relationships. Aside from such extremes, the formation of a digital psyche that thrives on online interactions may get in the way of human reasoning and decisions.

ARTIFICIAL INTELLIGENCE FOR BETTER DECISIONS

Bobbing up like a cork on turbulent waters, the human mind has the power to benefit from a torrent of digital content as well as an inspiring diversity of opinion. Indeed, a *learning mindset* of any individual, group, or organization will pivot on the determination to learn, adapt, and improve even in the face of setbacks. As the digital world brings exponentially more information than what was available in the past, a learning mindset represents a mental survival shift from the now ineffectual know-it-all mantra.

Basic learning-by-doing mechanisms can be illustrated with a sequential technique in artificial intelligence known as backtracking. It resolves challenges like finding the center (or exit) within a maze. As the computer reaches the end of an open path, it reverses its steps back to the last bifurcation point.

Backtracking has the wisdom to keep track of the path just explored and the undeterred perseverance to try another unexplored open path. Backtracking algorithms succeed when they reach the expected target within the maze or otherwise stop after having exhausted all open paths. Would digital learning always require such a tedious trial-and-error approach?

Artificial intelligence dispels the human notion that the apparent and first conceived solution to a complex challenge is the only or most appropriate one. As a simple example, a maze may have several possible exits. In many complex challenges, the existence of more than one solution may seem to be counterintuitive.

To the extent that the problem at hand can be represented as maze-like pathways or a network of nodes, calculations from graph theory may reveal the total number of possible independent paths leading to the end state or solution. In many situations, the calculated (and combinatorial) possibilities would largely exceed the first impression. How can digital intelligence help in navigating such counterintuitive combinations and possibilities?

Advanced techniques in artificial intelligence, such as using heuristic values to estimate and adjust the expected chances of success for an open path in the maze example, may accelerate the resolution. And more advanced cognitive algorithms may tackle any given maze-like challenge more expeditiously. They are based on well-trained models using data from previous experimentations or supervised learning with representative examples.

The underlying neural networks would encapsulate the acquired knowledge and may greatly optimize the selection of open paths based on their probability to reach the goal. The potential of this kind of deep learning capabilities can go well beyond resolving maze-like problems. One of the pitfalls to overcome, much in the same way as with human learning, is the propensity to develop a bias. Digital bias stems from the accumulation of skewed patterns in training sets or acquired knowledge.

Quantum computing is a most recent and advanced digital technology that may be employed to tackle complex maze-like challenges instantly, thoroughly, and possibly in one single try. The power may seem a bit too pretentious to grasp, particularly to people who got mired in complex problems or have already enjoyed the effectiveness and speed of state-of-the-art artificial intelligence techniques.

For starters, quantum computing runs on multiple parallel q-bits operating at deep subzero speeds. Quantum computing is therefore much faster than the binary (0-1 bits) processors underpinning electronic computers.

The logic behind quantum computing builds on a property of quantum physics known as superposition. In lay terms, a quantum algorithm could overlay all possible paths naturally and calculate their fitness to resolution in just one go. The opportunities in complex fields, such as health sciences, are enormous.

Despite all the wisdom and cognition capabilities of artificial intelligence, and notwithstanding the mighty seer power of quantum computing, these advanced techniques are far from perfection. Opposite the digital world, human behavior and real-life situations may complicate the ability to find solutions and arrive at most effective decisions.

Circumstances change dynamically and may do so steeply due to viral swings. Reality may overwhelm the best models and fastest computing algorithms. Even the laws of physics may follow different approaches when looking at inertial, steady systems versus accelerating motions. At extreme speeds, special relativity phenomena may alter the conventional notion of space and time.

In capital markets, broad financial distress and widespread investor gloom may break the steady equilibrium between offer and demand and cause a systemic downfall or painful recession. High-speed algorithmic trading requires digital circuit-breakers to prevent a position, or the entire market, from crashing when confronted with unusual imbalances.

Digital disruption may also alter the market dynamics. For example, chatbots and digital agents may help investors, and their financial advisors, ponder buy or sell opportunities based on personal situations, market trends, or sudden events. In a collective digital paradigm, what would then be the driving force that is known as investor sentiment? Would it be the propensity of individual investors, the wisdom of the financial advisors, or a lurking bias in the digital agents? Under distressed market conditions, could investors still trust a digital agent?

A GLIMPSE INTO FUTURE DECISIONS

Cognitive and robotics science keep making strides toward autonomous thinking. As illustrated in *Exhibit 12*, computing has been making noticeable progress along the way. Self-driving cars provide a current example of the advances in autonomous reasoning.

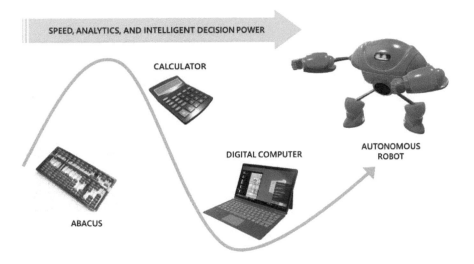

SPEED, ANALYTICS, AND INTELLIGENT DECISION POWER

CALCULATOR

DIGITAL COMPUTER

AUTONOMOUS ROBOT

ABACUS

Exhibit 12 – From the abacus to the robot

Autonomous vehicles can digest simultaneous input from multiple sensors in real time and take appropriate action within milliseconds. Commercial smart cars have already deployed diverse digital driving features such as lane departure warning and adaptive cruise control. Besides these seemingly mechanical cognitive and perceptual capabilities, could computers learn by themselves?

Perhaps it is worth bearing in mind the Turing test or imitation game that was mentioned earlier in this chapter. In Turing's game, a computer would try to persuade an interrogator that he or she is interacting with a human being. In a similar vein, an unsupervised learning technique used in artificial intelligence, known as adversarial neural networks, seeks to make cognitive networks smarter.

The process sets up a challenger neural network to generate a multitude of ambiguous and confusing patterns to fool another (discriminating) neural network that has the task to discern and interpret specific images. Similar to the relentless punches thrown by a boxing spar, such exhaustive adversarial digital training ends up improving the learning acquired by the neural network.

Another technique that advances such autonomous intelligence is known as reinforcement learning. In this scheme, an intelligent software agent generates random explorative scenarios to try out and gauge the established goals or rewards.

Reinforcement learning algorithms do not assume knowledge of an exact mathematical model, and thus differentiate from basic control theory programming methods and Markov decision processes (Wikipedia, n.d.). This random exploration process yields alternative strategies and autonomous action paths that would surpass the supervised learning from experts or unsupervised training using a representative set of practical examples.

As autonomous computing may learn faster and farther than human reasoning, caution must be taken to avoid illogical inferences and unpredictable behaviors. In most cases, digital evolution algorithms may discover innovative and legitimate alternatives that bring much better outcomes than what human experts would typically expect. In a similar fashion, unencumbered (and tireless) digital exploration and learning may overcome the intrinsic bias of the human mind.

Opposite their ability to open new dimensions of performance and find breakout action paths, autonomous systems might bring new vulnerabilities and unintended consequences. Hence the importance of maintaining a human loop amid all the artificial intelligence logic to preserve common sense, ethics, and integrity.

A dramatized situation was featured in the film *War Games* (Badham, 1983), where a teenage hacker accidentally gets an autonomous military supercomputer to engage in global thermonuclear war, thinking it was just an electronic game. As computing power and digital ingenuity continue thrusting forward, artificial intelligence must keep in touch with human realities.

REALITY BECOMES DIGITAL

Since the days of the abacus, humans have had to learn how to operate manual, mechanical, and digital computers. As artificial intelligence has most recently gotten close to human parity in several cognitive dimensions, the time has come for technology to adapt to humans. Virtual reality has represented a first step in that direction. Whereas virtual reality gaming has gained popularity thanks to relatively inexpensive and immersive visors, this technology has been around for several decades.

Airlines have been employing sophisticated and realistic virtual reality montages of aircraft cockpits, known as flight simulators, to train their pilots for many years. Such contraptions are mounted on high performance hydraulic mechanisms that simulate the aircraft bank, pitch, and multidirectional acceleration. As seen in the film *Sully* (Eastwood, 2016), pilots have an impressively real view from the cockpit and can fly the simulator by interacting with practically the same array of gears and devices offered in the real plane.

To assist humans with visualization and understanding, augmented reality technologies can overlay relevant on-screen information that is projected over a see-through screen. Nowadays, a practical example is found in the digital heads-up displays that are featured in some cars. In such displays, drivers may visualize, dynamically directly through the windshield, selected travel parameters related to the speed and driving directions. Another example would be the gaming hype of Pokémon™ Go (The Pokémon Company, n.d.) where gamers walk around their real surroundings catching virtual creatures on their smartphones.

Still, newer mixed reality technologies such as HoloLens (Microsoft Corporation, n.d.) provide an immersive digital interaction experience for business and industry. By wearing an open headset that is equipped with computing power, artificial intelligence software, and spatial sensors, people can overlay realistic, three-dimensional holograms over their open field of view. How real can mixed reality appear?

Operators can combine holograms and real objects and add augmented analytics and insights. The ability to track the movements of the hands and eyes enables an operator to move the holograms around as if they were real objects (and resize them at will).

Mixed reality applications may fulfill diverse purposes, such as remote expert hands-on advice, simulation of delicate operating room procedures, digital twins for industrial equipment maintenance, and architectural or engineering design. Mixed reality may help financial decision makers with a holographic, intelligent representation of capital markets instruments and virtual screens while operating a cluttered array of physical computer screens.

REFERENCES

Amershi, S. (2019). *Guidelines for Human-AI Interaction.* Retrieved from Microsoft Research: https://www.microsoft.com/en-us/research/uploads/prod/2019/01/Guidelines-for-Human-AI-Interaction-camera-ready.pdf

Badham, J. (Director). (1983). *WarGames* [Motion Picture]. Retrieved from https://www.imdb.com/title/tt0086567/

Dalio, R. (2017). Principles. New York: Simon and Schuster.

Eastwood, C. (Director). (2016). *Sully* [Motion Picture]. Retrieved from https://www.imdb.com/title/tt3263904

Feigenbaum, E. (1993). DENDRAL: a case study of the first expert system for scientific hypothesis formation. *Artificial Intelligence*, 209-261.

Godard, J.-L. (Director). (1965). *Alphaville* [Motion Picture].

Retrieved from IMDb: https://www.imdb.com/title/
tt0058898

Ifrah, G. (2001). *The Universal History of Computing: From the
Abacus to the Quantum Computer.* New York: John Wiley
& Sons, Inc.

Johnston, I. (2002). *Aeschylus - Oresteia.* Retrieved from Vancou-
ver Island University: https://malvma.viu.ca/~johnstoi/
aeschylus/oresteiatofc.htm

Lehman, J. (2018, August 14). *Cornell University.* Retrieved from
arXiv:1803.03453: https://arxiv.org/abs/1803.03453

Marguin, J. (1994). *Histoire des instruments et machines a calculer.*
Paris: Hermann.

Microsoft Corporation. (n.d.). *HoloLens 2.* Retrieved from Microsoft: https://www.microsoft.com/en-us/hololens/

Microsoft Research. (2019, February 12). *Everything you always
wanted to know about extreme classification (but were
afraid to ask).* Retrieved from Microsoft Research Blog:
https://www.microsoft.com/en-us/research/blog/every-
thing-you-always-wanted-to-know-about-extreme-classif-
ication-but-were-afraid-to-ask/

Minsky, M. (1974, June). *A Framework for Representing Knowledge.*
Retrieved from MIT Media Lab: https://web.media.mit.
edu/~minsky/papers/Frames/frames.html

Murphy, B. (1996). *Nineteen Eighty-Four - Benét's reader's encyclopedia.* Retrieved from Wikipedia: https://en.wikipedia.org/
wiki/Nineteen_Eighty-Four

Pascal, B. (1645). *La Machine d'arithmétique.* Retrieved
from Wikisource: https://fr.wikisource.org/wiki/La_

Machine_d'arithmétique

Stanford University. (2016, September). *Artificial Intelligence and Life in 2030*. Retrieved from One Hundred Year Study on Artificial Intelligence: https://ai100.stanford.edu/2016-report

Swade, D. (n.d.). *The Babbage Engine*. Retrieved from Computer History Museum: https://www.computerhistory.org/babbage/engines/

The Myers & Briggs Foundation - excerpted with permission from the MBTI° Manual: A Guide to the Development and Use of the Myers-Briggs Type Indicator°. (n.d.). *MBTI° Basics*. Retrieved from mbti: https://www.myersbriggs.org/my-mbti-personality-type/mbti-basics/

The Myers & Briggs Foundation. (n.d.). *MBTI° Basics*. Retrieved from mbti: https://www.myersbriggs.org/my-mbti-personality-type/mbti-basics/

The Pokémon Company. (n.d.). *Pokémon Go*. Retrieved from https://www.pokemongo.com/en-us/

Turing, A. M. (1937). On Computable Numbers, with an Application to the Entscheidungsproblem. *Proceedings of the London Mathematical Society*, 230-265.

Turing, A. M. (1950). Computing Machinery and Intelligence. *Mind*, 433-460.

Wikipedia. (n.d.). *Reinforcement learning*. Retrieved from Wikipedia - The Free Encyclopedia: https://en.wikipedia.org/wiki/Reinforcement_learning

6.
DIGITAL VALUE-ADDED SERVICES

WHAT DIGITAL CUSTOMERS WANT

EARLY IN THE TWENTIETH CENTURY, a primary need of bank customers revolved around having a safe place to keep their money (mostly deposited and withdrawn as banknotes). Then the demand grew for the ability to issue paper checks as payment from their checking accounts (usually maintained as physical ledgers). Banks would pay some interest to entice customer savings. Getting a bank loan guaranteed against salary, commercial, craft, industrial, or professional earnings represented another salient customer need. Banks would intermediate between depositors and lenders and gain an interest rate margin.

The spread in foreign exchange transactions also provided an attractive revenue source for banks, as customers needed to buy or sell diverse currencies. Banks would, however, put more resources and sophistication into corporate and commercial banking activities, as these brought the larger share of revenues.

Trade finance and institutional investments may serve as classical examples of such lucrative wholesale activities. Does a product mix of paper-based banking products sound rich enough? The advent of digital technologies and sophisticated customer demands gave rise to more complex banking scenarios.

The centuries-old bank service culture was hampered by an authoritative and reactive stance. It was rooted in the commercial credit approval culture whereby banks had the power to turn down risky or unprofitable customers. Global economic growth coupled with competition in the digital world prompted banks to adopt a much friendlier and customer-focused posture.

Figure 11 – Digital customer services

This was essential to grow and keep a thriving consumer business segment. Banks would derive significant profits from auto, mortgage, and personal lending. Consumer deposits and savings would provide a cheap source of funds. Donning a most approachable *good neighbor* touch, smaller institutions like community banks and credit unions stood out for their personal service to consumers, members, and small businesses.

The era of digital plastic cards, initially equipped with a magnetic stripe and currently with a computer chip, would significantly change the profile and relevance of individual bank customers. Ubiquitous ATM machines and point-of-sale terminals as well as consumer spending habits brought a marketing Nirvana to the banks.

Digital consumer payments grew exponentially and carried the banking reach well beyond the confines of traditional bank branches. Banks would now mine a wealth of data about individual preferences, spending habits, and transaction location. However, banks lagged far behind when compared to the consumer intelligence that the retailer and manufacturing industries put to good use.

DIGITAL SATISFACTION?

Customer satisfaction is a widely accepted indicator of how well companies cater to the needs and expectations of their customers regarding the quality of products and services provided. As reflected in *Exhibit 13*, the American Customer Satisfaction Index (ACSI, 2019) compares a representative selection of typical banks against high-performing consumer goods and personal computer companies as well as the credit unions sector.

A seemingly complacent banking sector has fared slightly better than the individual satisfaction indexes from Bank of America and Wells Fargo shown in the exhibit. However, banks seem to be at a disadvantage when compared to the leading consumer industries. Absent a proactive attention to their customer needs and wants, digital technologies may broaden the satisfaction gap.

Exhibit 13 – American Customer Satisfaction Index (1995–2018)
Source: ACSI

The internet and digital mobile devices have augmented the depth, quality, and quantity of digital customer data and behaviors through myriad interactions and transactions by an order of magnitude. A continuing growth in the richness and pervasiveness of digital customer data is exacerbating the call to banks to do much better at understanding the consumer market. Fortunately, computer power and advanced analytics enables banks to go deep. Opposite the advances by other industries, the fundamental question that banks need to answer is: what do digital customers care about?

For the past few decades, banks have been mired in a never-ending quest to improve key performance indicators, such as operational efficiency, product profitability, and credit quality. Many banks are finally rediscovering their most valued asset: the customer.

Figure 12 – Rediscovering the customer

Customers are often referred as clients, particularly in capital markets firms, or members, which is rightfully the case for credit unions. Consumers now reign in the digital world, where a plethora of products and services from multiple providers are available with just one click. And banks, as well as other providers, get flooded with torrents of detailed information about the online behaviors and preferences of digital customers.

By mining these vast pools of digital information, banks are beginning to understand what performance attributes may really matter to digital customers. As customers may shop online for the best offers, their deciding factors would go well beyond the interest rate spreads that a given bank may strive to optimize.

And the trustworthiness of a bank just happens to be assumed. Most surprisingly, the most impactful differentiation influencing customer decisions for digital services hinges on intangible factors. For example: agility, innovation, speed, and personalization, all as perceived by each individual customer.

The Kano model (ASQ - American Society for Quality) may help in putting these digital factors in perspective against the traditional bank performance parameters. In the 1980s, Dr. Noriaki Kano (Wikipedia) isolated and identified three levels of customer expectations that impact customer satisfaction, namely:

- Excited needs
- Normal needs
- Expected needs

When applying this model to modern banking services, it becomes clear that many of the attributes that banks have traditionally been focusing on have become merely table stakes. Yes, regaining and maintaining customer trust is important but only caters to needs that customers customarily expect.

It is the same with financial product features, such as interest rates or fees. In a digital market most customers would feel normal shopping for fair and competitive prices. To avoid customer dissatisfaction, banks must execute these expected features well.

It may well be that traditional financial products and their performance had their moment in the past as effective differentiators. Customer perception of normal needs, and even excited needs, would, however, shift over time.

As customers may grow accustomed in the long run to some of the exciting attributes, these would go down in the Kano hierarchy and turn into normal needs or even expected needs. As depicted in *Exhibit 14*, the set of attributes that presently excite customers and serve as differentiators are influenced by technology-savvy providers of digital services, whether these are financial or not.

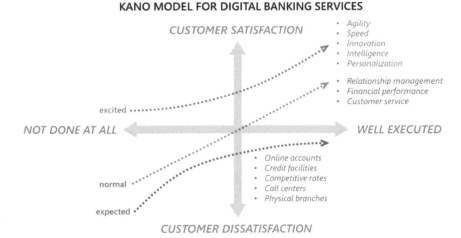

Exhibit 14 – Kano model for digital banking services

When customers do not get whatever attributes they expect, dissatisfaction takes hold. Dissatisfied customers are much more likely to moan about their bad experience than satisfied customers telling others about a good one.

Sometimes, dissatisfaction is so pronounced that irked customers may react with a gross comment or gesture. In America, such type of gesture is vulgarly known as *giving them the finger*. If this type of aggressive reaction may occur during people's daily life tribulations, would it also apply to service interactions?

Customer dissatisfaction has consequences. Unfortunately, bad personal service may beget bad behaviors. For instance, in an overcrowded airport due to massive flight cancellations and delays caused by bad weather, impatient and unpolite passengers may react with abusive language, tone, or gestures against otherwise well-intended but circumstantially overwhelmed airline personnel.

Another example is portrayed in the movie *Jerry Maguire* (Crowe, 1996): the deeply concerned son of an injured football player is complaining to his sports agent. The player had suffered concussions after several hits and was hospitalized, recovering from a bad one. When the agent responds insensitively about putting the player back on the field, the kid reacts with the finger gesture. Indeed, the expectation was that agents should care about the safety and well-being of their customers. In the film, this act of dissatisfaction served as a wakeup call for the agent, who then embarks on a humanization quest.

In banking, as well as retail services, dissatisfied customers may *walk with their feet* and do business with a competitor next door. As digital lifestyles change the banking interaction paradigm, unhappy customers may *walk with their fingers* right away and go for the app of another bank in their browser or mobile device. In digital services, leaving a provider after a bad experience is only one click away.

INNOVATIVE FACTORS OF DIGITAL VALUE

Digital services are shifting the expectations of banking customers, and some banks may have still to fathom the relevance of this shift. As a multitude of digital providers pervade banking with innovative offerings, constant change is becoming the norm.

Digital providers strive continually to address the evolving needs of digital customers as well as experimenting with, and probing, future excited needs that customers have still to articulate. This is exactly where agility comes in play. If any such futuristic features fail to land well with customers, providers must incorporate the feedback and adjust their offerings rapidly—almost instantly.

Given the competitive and open nature of digital services, time to market and the ability to ramp up customers fast are key to success. Besides such frequency and immediate availability to produce digital innovations that surprise and delight customers, the attribute of speed has a fundamental connotation.

Customers have abundant digital services at their disposal and may interact simultaneously with several providers. Whether these services are meant for work or pleasure, such abundance may appear to be a bit overwhelming to most people.

A MATTER OF SPEED

Slow response times and sluggish internet connections may disappoint customers and consume their precious time. With so many digital things to do, making good use of their time is indeed one of the attributes that customers appreciate the most.

This time attribute deserves extrapolating well beyond the short-lived attention that customers would pay to the ebb and flow of such fashionable, and rapidly fading, digital services. Multi-threading, intense bursts of point-in-time thrills set the stage for the digital customer experience overall.

The continual succession of flashes of digital experiences may occupy significant chunks of customer time every day. It is then worth asking how the aggregate of daily digital interactions fares against the life span of a typical person. Would digital natives end up spending over 60 percent of their valued time riding on digital thrills? Or could digital interactions add up to perhaps more than 80 percent of their total time?

In a nutshell: speed will be essential for digital services and their purpose. Given the advances in artificial intelligence, digital services may be tailored appropriately and scheduled in a most timely fashion to meet and excite the increasingly demanding needs of every customer.

Multifaceted digital services will address the personal well-being and healthy lifestyle needs and preferences of everyone. Banks and other providers of digital services should find ways to allow their customers to make the most of their time.

DIGITAL FEEDBACK

Besides the growing stature of speed as a key attribute of customer delight, banks should also find additional ways to wow digital customers. With the mounting preponderance of highly customizable digital interactions, providers may no longer have to standardize offerings as one size fits all.

Digital features that may delight one customer might fall flat with others. The reverse also holds true: whatever features seem to work for most customers might turn off a given individual. Facing an overwhelming variety of digital services, individuals have greater power to choose.

This means that digital providers must personalize their services to match the needs of each segment of one. Or, to put it in its reciprocal form, the richness of digital feedback about the behaviors and choices of each customer is driving digital providers to hyper-personalize their services.

Fortunately, machine-learning algorithms can plow rapidly and most effectively through many billions of customer digital feedback signals and enable such ultra-granular segmentation. And predictive analytics can single out what would be the best next action to be recommended to an individual customer in a specific situation.

Figure 13 – Digital feedback signals

Thanks to GPS capabilities, beacons, or wireless triangulation technology, mobile devices can pinpoint and track the actual location of the subscriber. Then live location information adds a creative variable to digital services.

Providers are orchestrating apps and services that help mobile customers with location tasks, such as finding the nearest bank branch or an open parking space. And in reverse, providers such as Uber drivers can find their customers at the designated pick-up point. However, location-aware services impinge on privacy requisites and require some sort of digital consent from the customer.

What would be so valuable to customers that may justify relinquishing the privacy of their location? Is it just the convenience and speed of the location-enabled service? In the case of Uber and other driver services, it may be argued that customer control and information are significant value factors.

DIGITAL CAR SERVICES

A few decades ago, and before the era of mobile phone or radio communications, catching a taxi could be a testing task. On rainy days or during busy hours, customers had to face uncertainty and possibly wait for a rather long time until an available taxi showed up. The odds worked against the passenger to be successful, and sometimes called for the customer to walk to a location with higher probability of finding a taxi.

Radio taxis changed the paradigm somewhat, as customers could call a dispatcher who would then contact the nearest available taxi and direct it to the pick-up location. Radio, and later, mobile phones evolved the taxi experience. Calling a radio taxi was practically as effective, convenient, and timely as contacting a private car service company. Except for the occasional nuance of having to deal with unwieldy dispatchers or procrastinating drivers, passengers gained some control of the process.

Powered by location and crowdsourcing features, digital car services are giving customers even more control. Passengers decide when and where to start the ride, and competing drivers respond to the call. All for the price of the privacy of their location and mobile app usage data, and at a lower cost, in most cases.

Most importantly, passengers get rich information about the ratings of the responding driver and live data on the real-time location of the car and its likely time to reach the pick-up point. Such transparent, live information helps shorten the perceived duration of the pick-up process. It also puts riders further in control, as they have the option to cancel the ride at any time before it starts.

Intelligent services follow a similar pattern: instead of customers having to find an available provider, the digital service will come to the customer. Customer satisfaction, starting as exciting innovative features and gradually becoming expected capabilities, hinge on the agility, convenience, cost efficiency, speed, control, and undeterred information transparency that digital services may provide.

Hence, the emerging paradigm of digital bank branches. As digital branches automate and extend the physical bank branch, the service reaches the customer wherever they may be, and at the right time, whether they're at home, the office, or on the go.

Given the surge in digital transactions, particularly from mobile devices, many banks are rediscovering payments as a promising line of business. Why is it so? It may be argued that payments services represent an expected attribute within the broader spectrum of the financial services functions.

After all, customers deposit their monies or trust their investments to a financial institution with the absolute expectation to get such holdings back whenever they feel appropriate. What would be the motivation, besides this centuries-old expectation to get their money back, for getting banks and their customers somehow excited about electronic payments?

The digital economy is taking hold. That is the reason why electronic payments are back in vogue. As depicted in *Exhibit 15*, the fast-paced, always on, right here digital economy is driving banks to speed up the payments process.

As the volume of digital interactions reaches to a hundred times the number of financial transactions, they increase the pressure on payments to respond immediately. Customers keep clicking or tapping frantically on their digital devices to navigate through vast pools of live information and services. Whenever the navigation crystallizes on a decision, customers want the associated digital payment to keep pace in real-time.

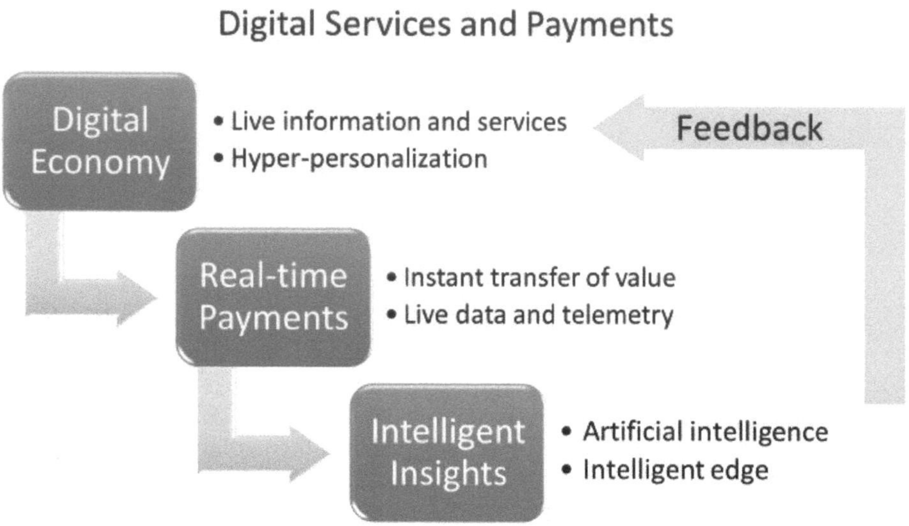

Digital Services and Payments

Digital Economy
- Live information and services
- Hyper-personalization

Feedback

Real-time Payments
- Instant transfer of value
- Live data and telemetry

Intelligent Insights
- Artificial intelligence
- Intelligent edge

Exhibit 15 – Digital services and payments

And the digital world conveys a wealth of information about the customer digital navigation whereabouts that triggered the payments transaction. Banks, oftentimes in combination with digital service providers, can mine all this information. Advanced digital capabilities, such as machine-learning algorithms, may further augment the value extracted from the customer interactions and their associated payments transactions.

And advanced digital devices now have the processing power and intelligence to close the feedback loop right at the point of presence. These intelligent devices can adjust dynamically and deliver custom services on the spot. Therefore, the power of intelligent cloud services is now extensive to advanced digital devices through what is called the intelligent edge.

DIGITAL BECOMING AUTONOMOUS

Intelligent devices are coming to life as everyday artifacts. In the higher end of the spectrum, for example, a new breed of digital dashboards is becoming commonplace in smart cars. Onboard navigation, music, and weather information tells of the diversity of digital services that may pop up on the dashboard, all seamlessly connected to a smartphone.

Other practical features include finding an available parking spot or requesting an appointment for servicing the vehicle, even starting a payments transaction. These features also include built-in alerts to assist in driving the vehicle and voice recognition. Ultimately, autonomous self-driving cars will be widely available.

All these gimmicks are powered by an increasingly intelligent array of integrated sensors, digital processors, and dependable connectivity. Artificial intelligence, such as cognitive services, are being pushed to digital devices that may operate autonomously.

SENSORS OF THE INTELLIGENT EDGE

New digital devices running in the intelligent edge are capable of recognizing faces and voices and even alerting instantly of situations that are captured on live video. They can respond to live gestures, allowing users to control the computer by moving their hands and fingers. Kinect (Microsoft Corporation, n.d.) serves as a versatile example of such cognitive devices.

The transportation industry provides some practical use cases of digital services. Electronic tickets have gained popularity with airlines, buses, and trains. Many airlines already offer passengers the ability to check in and obtain a digital boarding pass issued at their mobile devices.

In addition to the convenience of digitalization, these passenger services may connect with the airport traffic control system to track the live status of an incoming flight. Advanced apps, such as FlightAware (FlightAware, n.d.), may also show the actual position, altitude, and speed of a given flight—all available at the fingertips of the passengers.

As digital devices absorb increasingly rich quantities of information about people and their surroundings, wherever they may be, privacy concerns are escalating rapidly. Whereas customers may enjoy the intelligence of innovative and practical digital services, the flip side is that privacy matters too.

Many service providers are finding ways to strike a balance, for example, by being more transparent about what customer information might be captured and giving customers the choice to opt-in (or out) at will, anytime. European nations (EU GDPR.ORG, 2018) and other countries are already introducing regulations and procedures to protect individual data and privacy in the digital world.

Personal digital agents, acting with the required privacy on behalf of the user, represent a more advanced expression of proactive services. Like a genie out of the bottle, these personal services are always ready to assist and can alert their owners of a situation that deserves attention. Examples of digital agents are Alexa by Amazon (Wikipedia, n.d.), Siri (Apple, n.d.), and Cortana (Microsoft Corporation, n.d.). Would these and other innovative personal services build up the digital economy?

DIGITAL BUSINESS MODELS

Individuals do attach material value to actionable, hyper-personalized insights, that get delivered directly, swiftly, unobtrusively, and at the right time. However, vast availability, relentless innovation, and competition make it challenging for providers to monetize these digital services at face value. As the digital landscape evolves, customer purchasing decisions and market dynamics are giving rise to new models that shake up the established business management fundamentals.

Of course, digital companies are meant to generate sustainable profitability margins. The big news is that the time span that it takes a digital business to emerge, peak, and decline is shrinking fast. To achieve anything close to sustainable performance, digital businesses are adopting creative strategies.

Among a variety of ever-morphing strategies, it is worth calling out the following models:

- **Ecosystem**: thanks to open standards, digital providers may interconnect their specialized services to orchestrate a fuller, end-to-end, and more dynamic value proposition.
- **Digital content**: publishing and distributing copyrighted digital media such as books, movies, music, and television on demand.
- **Digital insights**: as customers attach value to information that is hard to find or figure out, they may pay for intelligent digital agents that can outperform humans in performing these tasks.
- **Aggregation**: putting together a combination of personal or topical information from diverse sources, such as the combined position of the customer financial accounts held by various providers.
- **Financial access**: artificial intelligence and crowdsourcing techniques are making borrowing and investments available to broader market segments on the spot.
- **Digital marketplaces**: as well-organized arrays of competing as well as supplementary services give customers the power of choice, such orchestrations attract customers and carry intrinsic value.
- **Lifestyle services**: intelligent personal digital devices, such as wearables, redefine the customer experience on health,

safety, sports, travel, and other everyday activities.

- **Augmented and mixed reality**: adding a digital overlay to headsets, visors, and mobile devices.
- **Accessibility**: intelligent apps and devices that empower individuals with disabilities to perform tasks (e.g. reading for the visually impaired) that would be otherwise pose a significant challenge.
- **Disruption and disintermediation**: finding blind spots in the traditional value chain that may be broken down into more efficient and better performing modules.
- **New value added**: hyperscale computing power and intelligence may fulfill ingenious and previously unattainable tasks, such as real-time risk analysis or rebalancing a personal investment portfolio.

In many modern economies, services industries have already been outperforming other sectors. For example, *Exhibit 16* highlights a few selected industries in the US, such as professional and business services ($ 4.3 trillion annual output), and financial services ($3.2 trillion annual output), which have been enjoying compound annual growth rates (CAGR) greater than 6 percent. These growth rates are significantly higher than those of traditional industries such as nondurable goods (3.5 percent CAGR) or construction (3.8 percent CAGR).

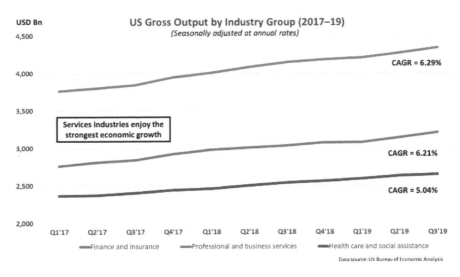

Exhibit 16 – US Gross output by industry group (2017–2019)

It is worth noting that in the private sector, the services-producing industries with an annual gross output of $24.9 trillion in 2019 (Bureau of Economic Analysis - U.S. Department of Commerce, 2020) greatly surpass the production of goods ($8.9 trillion). As consumers and businesses fuel an increasing demand for the services economy, digital technologies will further stoke this robust growth momentum.

Computer software and services have been rapidly adding value to the overall economy, and this trend is likely to accelerate further. In 2017, the total US digital economy amounted to $1.4 trillion, which represented 6.9 percent of the GDP. Indeed, the annual growth rate has been outpacing US economic growth by over 4.3 times (Bureau of Economic Analysis - U.S. Department of Commerce, 2019).

As depicted in *Exhibit 17*, the economic value created by computer systems design and related services in the US amounted to $360 billion in 2017. Additionally, and without counting internet delivery, digital technologies have been spurring new growth to the publishing industries (including software) at a clip of a 9 percent CAGR between 1997 and 2017.

Conversely, the growth rates for physical goods, such as computer and electronic products, have basically stalled. How will the advent of new breeds of digital services contribute to renewed economic growth?

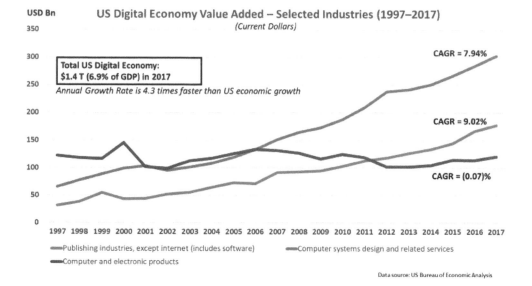

Exhibit 17 – US digital economy value added (1997–2017)

THE DIGITAL SERVICES ECOSYSTEM

This booming economy built on somehow intangible digital services seems to defy the very notion of the tangible value attached to physical goods. Among other substantial differences, the development and adaptation of digital services can move very fast.

In stark contrast to the cost and time involved in transporting physical goods, digital delivery is practically inexpensive and instantaneous. Advances in digital technologies brought another powerful differentiator: the almost universal interoperability embedded in open software standards.

How will this pervasive interconnectivity affect economic growth? First, virtually every development shop whether large or small may partake in the provision of digital services. A greater number of players ends up having a multiplying effect: the industry can turn out more and better innovations, faster. Next, a flurry of innovative digital offers creates new markets and builds up consumer expectations and demand for more sophisticated features. Last, a rapid fashion and fade cycle accelerates production and economic turnover.

So, the digital economy will require services providers to think and behave as an ecosystem. For financial services firms, the implications are dire. Not only will they need to inject intelligent technologies into their offerings but also partner with leading digital services companies.

As a matter of fact, many financial institutions have begun to form alliances with, take stakes, or acquire fintech companies. The future horizon, however, will drive them to think beyond the industry boundaries and find ways to interconnect with perpetually attractive and engaging non-financial digital services that capture the fancy of their own clients, customers, members, or prospects.

REFERENCES

ACSI. (2019). *Customer Satisfaction Benchmarks by Industry.* Retrieved from ACSI: https://www.theacsi.org/acsi-bench-marks/benchmarks-by-industry

Apple. (n.d.). *Siri.* Retrieved from Apple: https://www.apple.com/siri/

ASQ - American Society for Quality. (1980). *Kano Model.* Retrieved from ASQ: https://asq.org/quality-resources/kano-model

Bureau of Economic Analysis - US Department of Commerce. (2019, December). *Digital Economy*. Retrieved from Bureau of Economic Analysis: https://www.bea.gov/data/special-topics/digital-economy

Bureau of Economic Analysis - US Department of Commerce. (2020, January). *GDP by Industry*. Retrieved from Bureau of Economic Analysis: https://www.bea.gov/data/gdp/gdp-industry

Crowe, C. (Director). (1996). *Jerry Maguire* [Motion Picture].

EU GDPR.ORG. (2018). *EU General Data Protection Regulation (GDPR)*. Retrieved from EU GDPR.ORG: https://eugdpr.org/

FlightAware. (n.d.). *FlightAware*. Retrieved from FlightAware: https://flightaware.com/

Microsoft Corporation. (n.d.). *Azure Kinect DK*. Retrieved from Microsoft Azure: https://azure.microsoft.com/en-us/services/kinect-dk/

Microsoft Corporation. (n.d.). *Microsoft Cortana*. Retrieved from Microsoft: https://www.microsoft.com/en-us/cortana

Wikipedia. (n.d.). *Amazon Alexa*. Retrieved from Wikipedia: https://en.wikipedia.org/wiki/Amazon_Alexa

Wikipedia. (n.d.). *Noriaki Kano*. Retrieved from Wikipedia: https://en.wikipedia.org/wiki/Noriaki_Kano

7.
NATURE OF COMPETITION

WHAT ARE FINANCIAL SERVICES COMPETING FOR?

FOR CENTURIES, SOUND CAPITAL CAPACITY, sophisticated financial wisdom, and licenses from strict regulators have set aside banks, capital markets firms, and insurance companies from other industries. Will these pillars continue to serve as defining differentiators in the digital age? Would regulated balance sheets and specialized risk management capabilities determine the capacity to intermediate in financial markets? Not surprisingly, advanced digital technologies are democratizing the access to these capabilities in a manner that defies traditional incumbents.

For example, the instant syndication of credit through social media, commonly known as crowdfunding, is redefining the access to capital. And widely available online services provide state-of-the-art analytics, risk management, and intelligent decision support for financial transactions.

Similarly, a 360-degree view of all the consumer and enterprise digital activities is becoming more relevant than the intimate knowledge of the client, customer, or member finances. By the same token, financial regulators are openly encouraging the participation of digital entrants and challenger banks.

What will be the future differentiating factors to compete effectively? In the digital world, data, intelligence, and speed are the quintessential differentiators. And it may be argued that they all will combine with the emerging financial and non-financial capabilities of a rich ecosystem of digital providers, both from inside and outside of the financial industry. In a nutshell, effective differentiation will stem from the ability to deliver practical solutions and services to digital consumers or enterprises in a rich, timely, and well-orchestrated manner.

THE CHANGING NATURE OF COMPETITION

Digital Transformation has opened financial services markets to new competitors, both emerging businesses and, more recently, large technology and social media companies. These players have significant disruptive potential within the industry due to their size and digital capabilities, which they focus on providing frictionless experiences. "Incumbents—like banks and credit unions—are hardly standing still. In response to new competitive forces, they continue to adapt and evolve their own business models and digital capabilities" (Sievewright, The Changing Nature of Competition, 2019).

Additionally, the exploitation of data and analytics, and the use of artificial intelligence have created an explosion in the amount of data available. At the same time, cloud services and advances in technology are greatly increasing computing capacity so data can now be processed and exploited instantly by highly predictive tools. These new competitive forces and technologies have combined to create the most dynamic environment the financial services industry has ever known!

"At the intersection of finance and technology lies this amazing phenomenon, which has been accelerating the pace of change at a remarkable rate and is reshaping the industry's status quo, called fintech. With more than 50 percent of the global adult population using the internet to transfer money, pay bills, or shop online, fintech is no longer an emerging market: rather, it is an established industry with huge potential yet to be unlocked. New fintech entrants to the financial services industry see the opportunity to disaggregate the components of traditional 'banking' and offer targeted solutions with better service to consumers and businesses" (Sievewright, The Decade of FinTech, 2019).

As we look back upon myriad changes that have taken place in the financial services industry over the past decade, arguably none has been more impactful than the evolution of fintech. In fact, fintech has moved quickly from being a disruptive force to simply becoming the new norm.

No longer just disruptors, the so-called fintech *challengers* have grown into sophisticated competitors, and—in response—many financial industry incumbents have formed fintech partnerships and/or now offer fintech propositions of their own. Many fintechs are no longer start-ups: in many cases, they are mature, financially strong companies that operate at scale. A challenger bank born in Brazil, Nubank, reported twelve million customers with digital accounts in 2020 (Nubank, 2020).

FINTECHS, FINTECHS EVERYWHERE - AND FOR EVERYONE

Fintech has quickly become a global phenomenon that many refer to as the *fintech revolution*. According to market research, China is currently the biggest fintech market in the world, given its leadership position in the digital payments and alternative lending segments.

The US is the world's second largest fintech player and—due to the comparatively high disposable income of the US population and a high share of migrant workers—the US is a global fintech market leader in the personal finance segment. The market in Europe is smaller compared to China and the US. The leading fintech country in Europe is the UK.

At the heart of this fintech revolution has been the ability of fintech firms to substantially improve—and in many cases redefine—consumer and business service expectations and experiences. The relentless pressure on financial services firms to deliver seamless, convenient, and easy experiences to their clients, customers, or members has required them to think and act differently, including the pursuit of fintech partnerships.

Fintechs have built themselves using a convenience-led, design-first approach, supported by agile business processes. Unlike traditional financial services firms, fintechs have no legacy environments and design products and services with utmost agility from the vantage point of a clean-sheet-of-paper while keeping a technology-first mindset. At launch, these products and services are at once personalized, accessible, transparent, frictionless, and cost-effective.

THE FUTURE OF COMPETITION!

The financial services industry is undergoing its very own metamorphosis from which a new type of industry will emerge. New entrants with digital strategies and matching competencies will gain strength, while many incumbent firms—like credit unions—will be forced to alter their strategies to compete. As a result, there will be greater industry fragmentation and further blurring of industry boundaries.

The consumer experience will improve with each passing year. What seems to matter most to consumers and businesses these days is spending as little energy or effort as possible around financial services and these preferences will not change any time soon!

We are living in an era in which the very nature of competition in our industry is being redefined through a series of seemingly unrelated initiatives being taken by new entrants and some of the larger incumbents.

And, not by accident, fintechs redefined the rules of the game in financial services. What was considered new and disruptive five or six years ago has now become a prerequisite for all players, and financial services providers must place an unprecedented focus on their ability to differentiate themselves in retaining and attracting new consumers and businesses, whether by brand, price, delivery channels or execution.

DATA AS THE DRIVING FORCE? GOOGLE I.T.!

For all their focus and related investment in the financial services industry, fintechs do not have strong desires to turn into traditional financial services firms. They do not want the balance sheet or the risk, but what they are interested in is the data.

Fintech giants—such as Apple, Google, PayPal and the like—have unparalleled data analytics capabilities, which is something that a vast majority of traditional financial firms do not. Equipped with the right data, these fintechs can offer more sophisticated, highly personalized financial products and services than most traditional players can.

Google announced a new *smart checking* initiative. What new and innovative features will smart checking end up including? The public does not really know yet. Google is not sure either. And neither are its partners (Stanford Credit Union is one of them).

The project—code-named Cache—is envisioned as an extension of the Google Pay digital payments system. Interestingly, Google Pay is not winning the digital wallet race. In the past year, eMarketer has Google Pay mobile wallet adoption at roughly 50 percent of Apple Pay users. Given the launch and initial success of the Apple Card, which is very tightly integrated into the iPhone experience, Google might have felt compelled to announce something that would bolster the prospects of driving Google Pay volume.

Notwithstanding its somewhat blurry motives, Google's stated smart checking goal is to help consumers "benefit from useful insights and budgeting tools." The focus will be mobile-first users but the specifics of what will be offered are still being worked out.

Also, the financial institutions' brands (Citigroup is the other partner named so far) will be front-and-center on the accounts: Google will leave the financial plumbing and compliance to their financial partners. According to one Google executive, "Our approach is going to be to partner deeply with the financial system. It may be the slightly longer path, but it's more sustainable."

The initial industry response to Google's smart checking announcement was varied. The reaction tended toward tweets like "And so it begins..." alluding to the potential onslaught of Google and other technology firms onto the turf of banks and credit unions. And, Pymnts.com called it "the gasp heard 'round the world." That sentiment quickly shifted to comments like "Google isn't getting into banking—it's getting into banking data." It seems that for consumers, Silicon Valley giants are not after their money, they are after their data!

THE MORE THINGS CHANGE, THE LESS COMPANY VALUATIONS STAY THE SAME!

The nature of competition is changing at a phenomenal pace and nothing illustrates this better than looking at changes in rankings of the world's largest companies. Stating the obvious, it is the technology sector that is the key catalyst for change in the world.

Technology companies not only dominate our daily lives (how many times have you checked your iPhone today?) but also the ranking of the biggest companies based on market capitalization values. As illustrated in *Exhibit 18*, the change is especially dramatic when comparing company valuation data at year-end 2019 with valuations from year-end 2014 and 2009.

Top 5 Largest US Companies (2009–2019)

Company (EOY 2009)	Market Cap ($ B)	Company (EOY 2014)	Market Cap ($ B)	Company (EOY 2019)	Market Cap ($ B)
Exxon	330	Apple	652	Apple	1,300
Microsoft	269	Exxon	391	Microsoft	1,200
Wal-Mart	207	Microsoft	386	Google	933
Apple	189	Google	358	Amazon	924
Johnson & Johnson	179	Johnson & Johnson	293	Facebook	590
Procter & Gamble	179	Wells Fargo	286	J.P. Morgan Chase	432

Data sources: stockrow.com, macrotrends.net

Exhibit 18 – Top 5 US Companies by market capitalization (2009–2019)

Whereas ten- and five-years earlier oil and industrial companies were making the top five rank, by the end of 2019 only large technology companies dominated the scene. Some of these large technology companies seem to quickly gobble up any promising small company that could compete with them.

For example, Facebook has acquired upcoming threats WhatsApp and Instagram, while Google has made more than 120 acquisitions in the last ten years. Large banks, such as Wells Fargo and J.P. Morgan Chase scrapped the sixth place in 2014 and 2019 respectively however, technology companies now enjoy a much stronger growth momentum than financial institutions.

AND, THE FINTECH INDUSTRY SHOWS NO SIGNS OF SLOWING DOWN!

As if to emphasize the growing and substantial impact of technology companies, in 2018 the US fintech industry continued to grow and evolve with funding pouring into startups, more established fintech companies rethinking strategy, and incumbent financial institutions stepping up their technological developments.

Partnerships between fintechs and the financial institutions they once sought to displace are emerging. Also, we are seeing some fintechs broaden their reach or extend their value propositions. For example, various fintech companies are expanding from payments into digital lending and vice versa. Additionally, some are seeking to enter the business of banking more directly, such as Square.

Square has filed an application with the Federal Deposit Insurance Corp (FDIC) for a special Industrial Loan Company (ILC) license, that allows nontraditional financial firms to collect government-insured deposits. The bank would be Utah-chartered. Square—best known for its payment card readers—had first applied for banking charter in September 2017 but had subsequently withdrawn its application. In March 2020, the FDIC granted a license to the new unit, called Square Financial Services, which will offer deposit accounts and loans to small businesses.

FINTECH INVESTMENTS REACH NEW HIGHS

Additionally, venture capital-backed financial technology companies raised a record $39.6 billion from investors globally in 2018, up 120 percent from 2017. Funding was raised through 1,707 deals, up from 1,480 in 2017. The surge in funding was due in large part to fifty-two mega-rounds (investments larger than $100 million) which were worth $24.9 billion combined. Worth pointing out, though, is that a $14 billion investment in Ant Financial—the payment affiliate of Chinese e-commerce giant Alibaba Group Holding Ltd—accounted for 35 percent of total fintech funding alone last year.

Interestingly, 2018 also saw some new and bold fintech-related moves by two more traditional US corporations, namely Berkshire Hathaway and JP Morgan Chase:

- **Warren Buffett's Berkshire Hathaway** reached outside its closely followed investment playbook (which typically focuses on blue-chip American companies) by investing $600 million in two fintech companies focused on emerging markets and payments. Berkshire took a $300 million stake in Paytm—India's largest mobile-payments service that claims to have more users than PayPal—and bought shares in Brazilian payment processor StoneCo when it went public.
- **JP Morgan Chase's** Chairman and CEO, Jamie Dimon,

has been forthright about fintech's potential impact on the financial services industry. He is known to meet frequently with venture capitalists and entrepreneurs, touting his bank's huge investments in technology and warning (several years ago) that "Silicon Valley is coming with hundreds of startups with a lot of brains and money working on various alternatives to traditional banking." The bank has started its development of a new fintech campus for over 1,000 employees in Palo Alto, CA, one of the most expensive commercial real estate markets in the country. Sandwiched between Facebook and Google, the campus will be located at Stanford Research Park, home to Hewlett-Packard and Tesla, and on a plot of land formerly occupied by Lockheed Martin. This initiative follows the bank's acquisition last year of payments start-up WePay, a competitor to PayPal and Stripe in serving small businesses. WePay and its more than 275 employees will be moving to Palo Alto from the company's office in nearby Redwood City. Additionally, as Dimon said in his shareholder letter, the bank has almost 50,000 employees in technology and is pouring money into artificial intelligence and machine learning to reduce risk and improve underwriting, while also building up its cloud infrastructure.

2019: A YEAR OF INVESTMENT AND MEGA-DEALS

Certainly, the decade of fintech ended with an investment flourish and a series of mega-deals which emphasize the strategic importance of the category.

Cumulative global investment in fintech companies in the first three quarters of 2019— combining venture capital, private equity, and mergers and aquisitions—was more than $75 billion. As illustrated in

Exhibit 19, investments of $111.8 billion in the fintech sector in 2018 set a new record and a sharp increase over the $51 billion invested in fintech in the previous year (Consultancy.org, 2019).

From a financial services segment perspective, the payments and lending domains continued to attract the most significant investment globally. However, regtech has seen substantial growth over the past twelve months, increasing from $1.2 billion in 2017 to more than $4.5 billion in 2018.

Looking to the decade of 2020, however, the risk of geopolitical volatility and trade issues could jeopardize some of the recent growth seen in deal value and volume. Globally, there is likely to be an increase in investment focused on solutions targeted to the needs of the unbanked and underserved, especially in the developing world, including southeast Asia, Africa, and Latin America.

As investments flood in, the fintech industry is also experiencing unprecedented consolidation, with partnerships, deals, and acquisitions being made at a near-dizzying pace. In 2019 alone, three of the eight largest fintech deals of all time were announced, namely:

- **FIS's** $43 billion acquisition of WorldPay (Vantiv) – this deal (the largest fintech deal ever) combines one of the largest issuer processors, FIS, with one of the largest merchant processors, Worldpay. Thus, the new company will have data from both sides of the transaction. The deal also gives Worldpay an opportunity to quickly expand into large markets, such as Brazil and India, where FIS already has a presence.

- **Fiserv's** $22 billion acquisition of First Data – leadership of the combined Fiserv organization believes that, after realizing significant revenue and cost synergies, the company will generate $4 billion in free cash flow by 2022. Like the FIS acquisition of Worldpay, this new company will feature a huge market share in issuer processing, with First Data also having a large presence in merchant processing, especially with its popular Clover platform.

- **Global Payments'** $22 billion acquisition of Total System Services (TSYS) – Global Payments is a payment technology and software provider while TSYS provides payment processing, merchant services, and issuing to financial and nonfinancial institutions. The companies said the combined entity would provide its payment and software services to 3.5 million merchants and more than 1,300 financial institutions across more than 100 countries.

These impressive transactions are in addition to the dozens of smaller deals being made by the industry's larger players, such as PayPal and MasterCard.

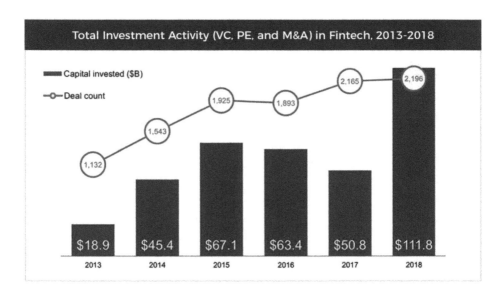

Exhibit 19 – Investments in fintech (2013–2018)
Source: Consultancy.org

While not all these mergers and acquisitions can be painted with broad strokes, it does appear many are defensive moves specifically taken as a reaction to the disruption that technology is bringing to the financial services industry. For instance, in the conference call following the announcement of the Fiserv and First Data merger, Fiserv's CEO Jeff Yabuki specifically called out Square for causing fear within the banking industry, serving as one of the catalysts for the First Data deal.

BIG PLAYERS PLAY THEIR PAYMENT CARDS

It is safe to say that five years from now the payments ecosystem will look vastly different because of continuing technological advances and innovations being driven by some of the largest technology and financial companies in the world.

Several examples are very worthy of close monitoring:

- **Apple** launched the Apple Card, positioned as a new kind of credit card designed to help consumers lead a healthier financial life. Apple Card is built into the Apple Wallet app on iPhone, offering consumers a familiar experience with Apple Pay and the ability to manage their card right on iPhone. Apple's Jennifer Bailey, Vice President of Apple Pay, commented, "Apple Card builds on the tremendous success of Apple Pay and delivers new experiences only possible with the power of iPhone."

    According to Apple, the Apple Card will transform the entire credit card experience by simplifying the application process, eliminating fees, encouraging consumers to pay less interest and providing a new level of privacy and security. Apple Card also offers a more compelling rewards program than other credit cards with Daily Cash, which gives back a percentage of every purchase as cash on consumers' Apple Cash card each day.

- On the debit card side of payments, **Bank of America (BofA)** launched a digital debit card and other enhancements to its mobile banking app designed to make it easier and more convenient for customers to manage their money. These latest enhancements further advance the company's *high-tech and high-touch* approach. BofA's new digital debit card has the same protections and benefits of a physical debit card and is immediately available in the mobile app to make payment in stores, in apps and online using a mobile wallet. The card can also be used to withdraw cash and make deposits at the bank's cardless ATMs. Commenting on this initiative, BofA's Head of Advanced Solutions and Digital Banking, David Tyrie, said, "Our goal is to bring never-before-possible convenience to clients' debit cards. Clients can transact immediately and avoid waiting for their permanent card. This feature is one of several new digital offerings that reinforce our commitment to making clients' financial lives easier." The bank's digital banking platform serves more than thirty-seven million digital clients, including more than twenty-seven million active mobile users. During the first quarter of 2019, BofA clients logged into mobile 1.5 billion times and deposited thirty-four million checks via mobile.

- **Facebook** is the dominant player in social media with more than two billion worldwide. This enormous scale comes with incredible power and—despite the intense regulatory scrutiny the company is under—few would doubt the depth of the company's resources today, whether financial, technological or the sheer number of so-called *eyeballs* served. Facebook made headlines with the launch of Libra— its proposed cryptocurrency—which will be operated with a consortium of partners, including global payments providers, credit card companies and consumer companies.

It is important to realize that Facebook is launching two cryptocurrencies: Libra, and the one available only to Facebook and its corporate partners, the Libra Investment Token. The former will be backed by a basket of fiat currencies and cash equivalents, which means that for every dollar of Libra in existence, there will be (in theory) a dollar's worth of real-world assets which that token may be exchanged for under certain conditions. A normal user would get $100 worth of Libra by spending $100. Libra can (again, in theory) be used across a variety of platforms or sent to an approved friend.

Regarding the Libra Investment Token, the Libra Association (a Swiss not-for-profit company) puts your $100 into a variety of low-risk, short-term investments like US Treasury bills. If one-month T-bills were yielding 2.125 percent on an annualized basis, the association would earn two dollars and change on a one hundred-dollar Libra purchase. Those funds are controlled and spent by the Libra Association. They are used first to fund the operation of the network with the remainder being divided among the Libra Investment Token holders according to their holdings, with policies determined by the association.

The association itself is made up of holders of the Libra Investment Token who invested a minimum of $10 million, as well as special impact groups selected by the association to have a vote but who do not have to buy the Libra Investment Token. Early investors are primarily large technology and venture capital companies for whom $10 million is not a huge investment.

Libra's future success—in the US at least—will be determined largely by how much share of the US money supply it can grab. In February 2020, M1 (which includes cash, coins, and money in checking accounts) stood at $4.0 trillion and COVID-19 relief packages bumped it up to $4.8 trillion in April. Looking, say, five years ahead, it is easy to imagine Libra securing a small percentage share of M1. But this small share would, in turn, generate huge financial returns for investors in the Libra Investment Token.

Libra appears to be a way to capitalize on Facebook's dominance of today's social media (and its partners' industries) to kick-start a real, global network effect around a new digital currency. If even a fraction of Facebook's user base converts to Libra, it is on the path to becoming the largest and most profitable *financial institution* (albeit decentralized) in the world!

CREDIT UNIONS BUYING BANKS

The ability to compete successfully in the financial services industry will be built on being able to achieve and leverage scale. The rapid (and continuing) consolidation of the credit union industry is a testament to this and, in addition to other constraints on their growth, credit unions have field-of-membership requirements. Restrictions on credit unions' field of membership have relaxed over time, giving credit unions more options for growth than ever before.

One way to grow, of course, is organically. However, a much faster way to grow is to purchase another financial institution and integrate it into existing operations. Historically, a vast majority of credit unions choosing to expand via acquisition have done so by merging with other credit unions. In recent years, however, there has been an increase in the incidence of credit unions buying banks. Indeed, *Exhibit 20* shows that while there was only one such transaction in 2012, there have been many more since.

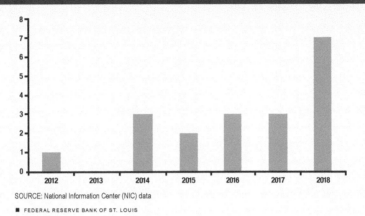

Credit Unions Purchasing Banks and Thrifts: Number of Transactions per Year

SOURCE: National Information Center (NIC) data

■ FEDERAL RESERVE BANK OF ST. LOUIS

Exhibit 20 – Number of transactions (2012–2018)
Sources: Federal Reserve Bank of St. Louis,
National Information Center (NIC)

Credit unions that have engaged in this activity include: Achieva Credit Union, Advia Credit Union, Avadian Credit Union, Evansville Teachers Federal Credit Union, Five Star Credit Union, Georgia's Own Credit Union, IBM Southeast Employees Credit Union, Lake Michigan Credit Union, Landmark Credit Union, LGE Community Credit Union, Mid Oregon Federal Credit Union, Municipal Employees' Credit Union of Baltimore, Royal Credit Union, Superior Choice Credit Union and United Federal Credit Union.

Credit unions will likely study the financial performance of these early adopters to determine whether to pursue their own bank deals. If the acquiring credit unions can successfully navigate the different cultures, regulations and business models, and if they can retain enough of the employees and customers (converting them to members), these transactions have the potential to be a win-win for all the stakeholders involved.

And yet, while time will tell whether credit unions will continue to buy banks at an increasing rate, it will likely never be a dominant transaction type, not least because of the various regulatory issues involved.

FINANCIAL INSTITUTIONS STAY PHYSICAL OR GO DIGITAL?

As we know, change does not come easily to financial services. Decades-old practices and the vast technology infrastructure (what we often call legacy systems) that supports them can prove to be huge barriers. This is both a blessing and a curse to industry incumbents like credit unions. The inefficiencies of current systems and practices associated with their infrastructure, and the intensive focus to create exceptional member experiences and value, are what attract potential disruptors.

Compared to the legacy core banking systems that still behoove the industry, fintechs have an edge in developing bespoke, unencumbered digital banking solutions using advanced technologies. However, having to build the necessary elements of broad financial services infrastructure from scratch is a barrier to disruptive players. Running a complex credit union takes enormous resources, as well as credibility and trust among members, third parties and regulators.

The dynamic between fintechs and traditional financial institutions—like credit unions—is shifting from disruptive competition to innovative collaboration. The rapid evolution of fintech presents credit unions with challenges and opportunities across a variety of domains. To remain competitive and relevant in today's marketplace, credit unions must consider whether to invest in new technologies, partner with fintech companies, or focus on existing services to further member satisfaction and growth.

The level of credit union-fintech collaboration needs to increase exponentially in the early years of this new decade. Credit unions are well-positioned to negotiate a constantly evolving technological landscape if they focus on their core mission of member service.

While a certain degree of disruption is inevitable, credit unions should be most concerned about fintechs that can emulate the same type of trust-based relationships common among community financial institutions, but on a national scale, whether through mobile apps or other novel technologies. The fintech space is moving to a new phase of collaboration and credit unions need to respond!

In this new world, traditional firms face the prospect of losing control as fast, easy, and simple digital experiences become the norm. However, thanks to technology advances, automation and greater focus on improving business processes, there will be greater efficiencies across-the-board, and firms that develop expertise in collaborating with an extended network of technology partners, fintechs and other entities will have more control over their destiny.

In essence, the digital transformation of the financial services industry has radically altered the nature of competition. The long-term impact of this change continues to be uncertain because, in part, it is dependent on future US regulatory and competition policy frameworks. However, one thing is granted: the financial services business model is under attack and, over the next five years, will change significantly—perhaps beyond recognition.

REFERENCES

Consultancy.org. (2019, February 21). Consultancy.eu Europe - News. Retrieved from Consultancy.eu: https://www.con-sultancy.eu/news/2390/global-fintech-investment-more-than-doubled-to-112-billion

Nubank. (2020). Nubank - Press. Retrieved from Nubank: https://nubank.com.br/en/press

Sievewright, M. (2019). The Changing Nature of Competition. Sievewright & Associates.

Sievewright, M. (2019). The Decade of Fintech. Sievewright & Associates.

8.
DIGITAL PAYMENTS

STEPPING UP THE TRANSFER OF VALUE

IN PREHISTORIC TIMES INDIVIDUALS, FAMILY groups, or mostly nomadic tribes used to find, produce, and store food, and craft clothing and utensils to attend their basic needs. Facing inclement weather and disease, and constrained by their own means, improving and sustaining the quality of life was the main challenge. After this nomadic epoch, people settled down in civilizations and engaged in direct and straightforward barter. By exchanging their own surplus of goods, or at least sharing some, civilizations learned how to maximize the value of their goods.

Barter sounds simple, doesn't it? People would sense the (mutual) demand for (surplus) goods and exchange them on the spot. And perhaps adjust for the relative effort, cost, or value of their respective goods. Therefore, a fair trade for a jug of milk might instantly fetch several ears of grain. More valuable goods, such as metals, gems, and specialty crafts and tools, would trade at a higher premium.

Three millennia ago, far before the invention of digital computers, metals, in the form of ancient coins, came to facilitate physical trade. Coins became the quintessential expression of money. "Ancient coins were more than just a means to exchange value, they were also monetary art" (GovMint.com, a brand of Asset Marketing Services, LLC, n.d.). So what is the point here? Right from the start, the perceived value of money transcended its monetary or trading equivalence.

Besides the intrinsic trade value of the metal or the prestige attached to the minted effigy, the coin might also have extra meaning. For example, if it was awarded as a prize, or during a memorable ceremony, or perhaps handed out by a notable authority or conspicuous figure. That is to say, the circumstances in which it was acquired might augment the perceived value of a coin.

Beyond the exchange of goods, coins would also pay for labor and a variety of services. Money made it easier to settle a variety of services, including those of a professional nature and break out from the limitations of barter. Hoarding coins was easier (and seemingly more tempting) than bartering perishable, bulky, or low-demand goods. Large, accumulated wealth could wield a colossal purchasing power.

Barter was a natural way to exchange goods. And coins became the most convenient payment method of that time. Street markets for money exchange emerged, where people could trade coins for coins.

Oftentimes the money exchange arbitrated the differential value between mints or currency from various origins. An unintended consequence stemmed from the market spread between bid and offer prices for the same type of coin. Arbitrage margins created a transaction gain for traders, however, the intrinsic value of money might fall short of justifying such extra added wealth.

Speculative trading margins plus the inflated power of accumulated wealth were among the many perils that behooved the generalized acceptance of coins. Unscrupulous traders would file some dust or scrape tiny pieces of precious metal from each coin.

Coins would represent a most convenient, lucrative, and vulnerable target. These value-draining approaches were already commonplace in the years before the Common Era. It took a millennium to see the first bank notes as accepted currency in a few international markets, as traders found it much lighter to carry paper rather than coins.

THE RISE OF DIGITAL PAYMENTS

For the most part of the twentieth century, paper dominated the commercial and financial worlds. Paper instruments took various shapes and forms as currency, financial instruments, transaction records, and supporting documentation.

In the 60s, with the advent of electronic processing, paper started to give way to digital transactions and records. As shown in Exhibit 21 (The Federal Reserve, 2019), the surge of debit card transactions and the steady rise of credit cards, over the past two decades, resulted in a sharp decline in the number of paper checks.

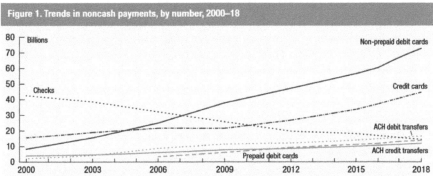

Figure 1. Trends in noncash payments, by number, 2000–18

Note: All estimates are on a triennial basis. Card payments were also estimated for 2016 and 2017. Credit card payments include general-purpose and private-label versions. Prepaid debit card payments include general-purpose, private-label, and electronic benefits transfer (EBT) versions. Estimates for prepaid debit card payments are not displayed for 2000 and 2003 because only EBT was collected.

Exhibit 21 – 2000–2018 Trends, Federal Reserve Payments Study

Source: The Federal Reserve

Among the key drivers for adopting digital processing were the noticeable gains in efficiency, global connectivity, speed, and transparency. But digital connectivity brought a new threat: cyberattacks and theft. Whereas companies and institutions have been strengthening their digital security continually, increasingly sophisticated attacks still pose a constant concern. In any case, digital payments have largely displaced paper.

Why would digital payments become so prevalent despite the continuing security threats? For starters, the immediacy of digital transfers drives this trend because indeed, time is money. And digital speed beats the lapse of several days that it would take to clear checks or other paper instruments.

A pivotal and distinctive advantage is that digital transactions convey other valuable information beyond the financial aspects of the payment. So digital payments stand out primarily thanks to their convenience and speed, right? There is more …

Here, it is important to draw an analogy to the extra value that could be attached to coins. By a similar token, digital payments may carry far more value than what merely transpires during the financial exchange: it is all about the context, purpose, and manner in which digital payments occur. The consumer context data is very rich thanks to exponential growth of digital services, coupled with the proliferation of ubiquitous broadband mobile access and mobile payments.

For example, information about the exact location where the payment is taking place, or which digital services were at play when the payment transaction got triggered. Also, the additional marketing value that may be attached to the transaction. The detailed information about the beholder and how the screen navigation led to the payment are valuable.

On the other side of this (digital) coin, it is important to highlight the consumer experience. Digital payments are much simpler and more tightly integrated into the purchasing of goods and services, especially when these happen to be digital too.

DIGITAL PAYMENTS BECOME EXPERIENTIAL

Payments transactions are becoming a most significant experiential interaction. It is all about facilitating the exchange of value at digital speed. Payments occur instantly, and in a manner that integrates seamlessly with whatever the parties to the transaction are doing, whenever and wherever they happen to be. So, value may change hands (literally, in the case of real-time, mobile person-to-person payments) at digital speed.

Figure 14 – Contactless digital payments

Whether a payment is person-to-person, or for example, several individuals splitting the bill at a restaurant, the transaction becomes a shared experience between the parties involved. Entities such as social media companies, crowdfunding schema, and the providers of mobile services are also playing a role as originators of digital one way and multi-way payments.

Hence, digital payments may readily engage several family, friends, or business participants. In a social setting, the experiential value of a payment transaction gets multiplied by a factor of at least two.

Multiple parties may partake in a series of convenient, fluid, swift, and transparent digital payments transactions. Then, such positive experiential habits end up building trust and nurturing the relationships among the participants. And the means that people choose to carry out such payments will become a key factor in the quality of the experience and the value to their relationship.

Novel ways in which bilateral or multi-way payments get originated, executed, and settled will acquire significant relevance. The speed, friendliness, and trust of digital payments attain new value dimensions that rival the financial parameters of the transaction.

In a social media context, people may appreciate the ability to attach memorable images, short videos, friendly text, or emoticons to a digital payment. Besides such social media scenarios, the flexibility to attach digital media to retail payments may add a subtle whiff of humanity and personal touch to otherwise stale business-to-consumer transactions.

These continual and pervasive digital experiences, together with the rich data that gets captured with each transaction, open a phenomenal economic potential. When aggregated across billions of digital transactions and relationships, such experiential value may compare to, or even exceed the monetary value that gets exchanged.

THREATS TO FINANCIAL STABILITY?

It is important to bear in mind the systemic perils and vices that arose with the transition of barter to currency transactions. Much like the cumulative power of currency, the augmentation and concentration of value by social media payment vehicles will carry new risks.

Freewheeling social media payments may bring collective potential but also threats. The foray of Facebook into the payments domain, coupled with its introduction of the Libra cryptocurrency consortium, tells of the disruption that digital payments bring to the financial services establishment.

Reaching to the far edge of these upcoming threats in digital payments, sudden surges in viral scams, global fraud, money laundering, organized crime, and massive monetary imbalances may end up compromising the stability of the financial system. These risks are too big to be left unchecked. Responding to the magnitude and transcending impact of such potential misuse, the emergence of pervasive digital payments will call for renewed industry discipline and regulatory twists.

REAL-TIME FOR REAL

Opposite a viral surge in digital payments and the additional experiential value that they convey, new threats are also rising. What truly haunts these vibrant real-time digital value transfer scenarios are something more mundane and harder to beat than all those sophisticated attacks or fraudulent scheme.

The harshest barriers to real-time processing are the old (read *legacy*) core systems that most financial institutions and the incumbent ecosystem of software services providers are still running. The predominantly batch-and-serial processing design of these systems prevents the completion in real-time of rich payment transactions. Besides the payment, digital transactions also carry a wealth of non-financial information about the parties and their point-in-time, attitude, and location context.

The total size of every digital transaction record falls right at the center of these legacy software shortcomings. Most legacy core banking and payments systems were designed primarily to represent a very narrow and elementary set of financial data.

For example, the account number and the bank routing number for both the sender and the beneficiary, the payment amount, the currency code, the transaction and value dates, and perhaps ancillary information such as any applicable interest or exchange rates might be contained in that set of data. The space reserved for data fields that carry other vital information, such as the names of the parties and references, may be fixed or severely constrained in size.

The need to connect with multi-party schema for clearing and settlement comes on top of the typical size constraints that legacy systems may impose. Such is the case of many automated clearing houses (ACHs) that still rely on end-of-day batch processing mechanisms. Which brings both unintended and well-intended consequences.

In typical legacy schemes, the intermediaries hold the funds of a payment transaction for a day or more to benefit from the financial float as the transaction moves along the payments chain. The sheer nature of end-of-day processing falls on the unintended side. What is worse, the business models of the various sender, correspondent, and beneficiary institution involved in a transaction represent the most visible and intentional barrier to real-time processing.

Given the financial intermediation margins and processing fees, many institutions have formed entire business units around the payment products. So real-time payments create a dire conflict for this rationale: should institutions relinquish the cherished float as a selfish benefit to tap the promising customer appeal, value, and volumes of real-time processing of financial and non-financial data?

From the end customer point of view, it may be argued that the enablement of a simple and exclusively financial payment transaction would merely carry a perfunctory value. In the simplest scenario, why would customers pay to access their own funds already on deposit with their financial institution?

Conversely, customers would appreciate many valued factors such as the anytime, anywhere enablement role of payments that are intended to fulfill purchases of goods and services. Or the extension of credit that may provide the liquidity to support a payments transaction. And most importantly, the experiential and informational aspects that end up making a digital real-time, seamless payment transaction either memorable or unnoticeable, whatever the case may be.

THE BUSINESS OF PAYMENTS

The business of payments is big business: global payments revenues have surpassed $2.3 trillion in 2018 and account for more than 40 percent of all retail financial services revenue, compared with just over 30 percent ten years ago. The payments business shows strong growth, fueled mostly by volume increases driving both transactional revenues (e.g. interchange) and liquidity revenues (e.g. net interest income).

The $2.3 trillion payments pie has been growing at around 8 percent over the past five years and the 2018 revenue flows look like this (Sievewright, Perspectives Report: The Future of Payments, 2018):

- $1.3 trillion from net interest income
- $0.8 trillion from interchange and other fee income
- $0.2 trillion from cross-border payments and trade finance-related activities

The macro trends evident in today's payments arena give every indication that incumbents—especially financial institutions—will need these strong growth tailwinds at their backs.

Legacy systems and business models usually suffer from further tribulations. The operational cost and burden of the related legacy business processes and established culture represents a most basic, albeit often overlooked, issue.

For every dollar in ineffective processing cost for legacy systems, the resulting operational cost overhead typically multiplies by about seven times. Reducing the total cost of business and technology legacy may heighten the opportunity to modernize and transform the aging core and payments systems.

For financial institutions, risk and regulatory imperatives also complicate the picture. For example, every payment transaction must undergo strict controls for anti-money laundering and manage the financial risks, such as credit, liquidity, and settlement that stem from virtually every legacy payments scheme.

Also, the ability to curtail fraud and protect, detect, and respond to malicious attacks is necessary in each transacation. In real-time processing, all mandatory controls and safeguards must take place concurrently with the payments. And financial institutions must have the means to report these activities in real-time too.

In a nutshell: to capitalize on real-time payments, financial institutions must encompass a broader value proposition beyond the financial aspects. Institutions should also seize the opportunity to fundamentally transform and rethink their legacy platforms and supporting capabilities.

MACRO TRENDS REDEFINING PAYMENTS

As the *payments* pie continues to grow, incumbents will need to prepare for an inevitable redistribution of revenues as the activities of retailers, social media giants, fintechs and other non-traditional payment firms result in:

- A disruption of traditional payment flows
- Innovation around new payment products and services
- An increasingly central role for these players in the payments business, globally

Exhibit 22 highlights other macro trends that we believe will redefine the payments business (Sievewright, Perspectives Report: The Future of Payments, 2018).

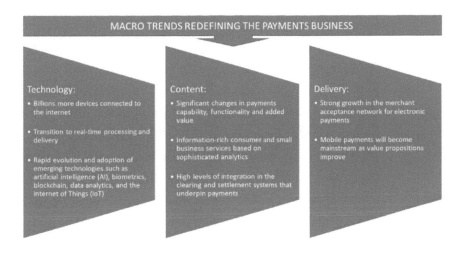

MACRO TRENDS REDEFINING THE PAYMENTS BUSINESS

Technology:
- Billions more devices connected to the internet
- Transition to real-time processing and delivery
- Rapid evolution and adoption of emerging technologies such as artificial intelligence (AI), biometrics, blockchain, data analytics, and the internet of Things (IoT)

Content:
- Significant changes in payments capability, functionality and added value
- Information-rich consumer and small business services based on sophisticated analytics
- High levels of integration in the clearing and settlement systems that underpin payments

Delivery:
- Strong growth in the merchant acceptance network for electronic payments
- Mobile payments will become mainstream as value propositions improve

Exhibit 22 – Macro trends redefining the payments business

Many of these macro trends are influenced by consumer experience and expectations. Digital transformation is making payments faster, cheaper, and more convenient. Over the next five years, mobile devices, supported by increasingly sophisticated technology applications, will accelerate the pace of change. Additionally, demographic shifts will not only increase demand for payment products and services but will require payment providers to substantially raise their game.

THE IMPACT OF DISRUPTORS

It is already clear that so-called *payments disruptors* are changing the payments landscape. Consider these examples (Sievewright, Perspectives Report: The Future of Payments, 2018):

- Amazon, Apple, Facebook, and Google have collectively built an impressive array of payments capabilities which drive mind-boggling transaction volumes.

- Apple's 2019 launch of the Apple (credit) Card will likely to be viewed by history as a pivotal event in the card services business. According to Apple CEO, Tim Cook, "The Apple Card completely rethinks everything about the credit card. It represents all the things Apple stands for. Like simplicity, transparency, and privacy. It builds on the incredible ease and security that millions of people love about Apple Pay. And it is the first card that actually encourages you to pay less interest. Whether you buy things with Apple Pay or with the laser etched titanium card, Apple Card can do things no other credit card can do." To launch the card, Apple partnered with Goldman Sachs, which had never issued a personal credit card in its history.

- PayPal and its subsidiary, Venmo, have defined the P2P payments market, securing massive market share (including within the much sought-after millennials segment), and creating new verbs along the way (e.g. "I will Venmo you!"). In the first quarter of 2020, Venmo processed $31 billion in net volume, up 48 percent from a year earlier (Statista, 2020). PayPal's efforts to make money from the Venmo P2P service have begun in earnest. The company hopes that Venmo users will start using their accounts to *pay-with-Venmo* as they shop for things online, enabling the company to earn transaction fees from merchants. And, we can expect to see PayPal introduce more dynamic checkout buttons that figure out whether a visitor/shopper is a PayPal or Venmo user and render the appropriate payment button(s).

- Square is building out a broad ecosystem of merchant and payment services. In March 2020, the Federal Deposit Insurance Corporation (FDIC) granted the company an industrial bank charter in Utah. Square will operate as a subsidiary of the bank and it is re-thinking its overall business strategy.

- Initiatives from several retailers are diverting interchange revenues away from card issuers: a good example is Target's RedCard offering consumers a 5 percent discount on all purchases. It is estimated that one out of every three payments to Target come through card issuers as ACH items.

But incumbents are not standing still and letting these so-called *disruptors* have everything their own way. One of the more notable initiatives is Zelle, which is a US-based digital payments network owned by Early Warning Services, a private financial services company owned by Bank of America, BB&T, Capital One, JPMorgan Chase, PNC Bank, SunTrust, US Bank, and Wells Fargo. The Zelle service enables individuals to electronically transfer money from their bank or credit union account to another registered user's bank or credit union account (within the US) using a mobile device or the website of a participating institution. Since its launch in 2017, Zelle has made impressive progress.

In 2019, $187 billion were sent through the Zelle Network® on 743 million transactions. Year-over-year payment values increased by 57 percent, while transaction volume increased by 72 percent. Nearly 500 financial institutions are contracted to participate on the Zelle Network. Further, it is estimated that more than 64 percent of US demand deposit accounts will have access to Zelle through the financial institutions contracted to join the Zelle Network.

US Consumers continue to adopt Zelle for everyday person-to-person payments, from paying their personal trainer, paying back a friend for last night's dinner, splitting costs while traveling, and gifting or sending and receiving funds for emergencies. Importantly, Zelle is built directly into each bank or credit union's mobile banking app, making the system very easy to use.

Additionally, the same real-time connection established for the participating financial institution can be used for other payments, such as account-to-account (A2A) transfers and bill pay. Zelle's early success is expected to continue and gain further momentum as it establishes itself as the mainstream P2P solution in the industry.

AND, HERE COMES THE FED!

In the US market, the Federal Reserve developed its Strategies for Improving the US Payment System paper (The Federal Reserve, 2017) which served as the catalyst for hundreds of organizations and individuals to come together to support making tangible progress against the five desired outcomes shared in the document, namely: speed, security, efficiency, international payments and collaboration.

In August 2019, the Federal Reserve Board announced that the Federal Reserve Banks will develop a new around-the-clock real-time payment and settlement service, called the FedNow[SM] Service, to support faster payments in the United States. The rapid evolution of technology presents a pivotal opportunity for the Federal Reserve and the payments industry to modernize the nation's payment system and establish a safe and efficient foundation for the future.

"The Federal Reserve believes faster payment services, which enable the near-instantaneous transfer of funds day and night, weekend and weekdays, have the potential to become widely used and to yield economic benefits for individuals and businesses by providing them with more flexibility to manage their money and make time-sensitive payments" (Sievewright, Perspectives Report: The Future of Payments, 2018).

Since its founding more than a century ago, the Federal Reserve has provided payment and settlement services, alongside and in cooperation with the private sector, as part of its core function of promoting an accessible, safe, and efficient US payment system. The

Federal Reserve has established over its history a broad reach as a provider of payment and settlement services to the more than 10,000 financial institutions across the country. That reach will help the FedNow[SM] Service support a nationwide infrastructure on which the financial services industry may develop innovative faster payment services for the benefit of all Americans.

In 2018, the board requested public comment on potential services that could be developed by the Federal Reserve to support faster payments. Of the more than 350 comments that took a position on whether the Federal Reserve should develop a new service for faster payments, over 90 percent supported the Federal Reserve operating an around-the-clock real-time payment and settlement service alongside services provided by the private sector. The board anticipates the FedNow[SM] Service will be available in 2023 or 2024.

Similar developments are becoming successful in other countries. For example, with the launch of its Faster Payments Service (FPS) in 2008, the UK initiated the global shift toward faster payments. This continuous, real-time clearing system includes several payment types as well as the following:

- Single, immediate payments
- Forward dated payments
- Standing-order payments
- Direct-corporate-access payments

Participating UK banks have been busy building customer-facing products and services that leverage the capabilities of the FPS including a product called Paym which enables customers of the participating banks to send and receive payments using a mobile phone number as a proxy. Some of the banks (e.g. HSBC) have extended Paym to business customers as well.

To achieve ubiquitous real-time payments in the US, the following outcomes will be needed:

- Industry collaboration around the creation of a faster payments ecosystem
- Federal Reserve settlement services that address the needs of a ubiquitous real-time retail payments environment
- A clear definition of the role of the Federal Reserve (beyond providing settlement services) in supporting the new and improved payments ecosystem

These outcomes—especially the collaboration task—represent a complex endeavor (to say the least) and pose huge challenges for participants.

OPEN BANKING - ALL CHANGE?

"2018 was a landmark year for Retail Banking in Europe as the impacts of the PSD2 (Revised Payment Services Directive – 2) are taking hold. Simply put, these rules—often referred to as *open banking*—replaced the original Payment Services Directive issued in 2008 and allow consumers to grant access to their banking and financial information to third parties aside from traditional banking institutions. The PSD2 rules cover the whole of the European Union" (Sievewright, Perspectives Report: The Future of Payments, 2018).

Basically, the new rules provide consumers with easier, more flexible ways to access their financial information, and more freedom and control over who they can share this information with. Consumers could access different online apps or services which can analyze their spending habits and provide money management advice or services. Consumers will also be able to switch account providers faster and easier than before, allowing them more freedom to pursue the best deals and offers.

Importantly, the rules also look to better protect consumers making online payments, help protect them from fraud, and allow payments across national borders within Europe without the need for complicated regulatory issues and processes.

The reason PSD2 has received so much attention in the US is that many view the regulation as a harbinger of things to come here. Already (almost as if they are preparing for similar regulation), several large US banks have started to open their data to third parties. While a PSD2 equivalent is an ocean away (literally) for the US, it is indicative of a trend that puts consumers in control over their own data and information.

THE EVOLUTION OF MOBILE PAYMENTS

Mobile payments encompass many different forms of payment, including near field communication (NFC), contactless solutions (using plastic cards or devices), e-wallets, P2P payments, and digital currency.

The evolution of smartphones and wearable technologies is enabling new payment capabilities. Also, the combination of innovations in security technologies—such as tokenization of card details, biometric-enabled multi-factor authentication, and EMV standards—and the availability of new readers at merchant locations, is producing a smorgasbord of payment options for consumers and the companies that serve them.

Also, the rise of connected devices will fuel strong growth in in-app purchases. Mobile apps will become increasingly sophisticated and consumers will be transacting via myriad new devices (some of which haven't been invented yet!). Innovative apps will create new value propositions for consumers and will also digitize cash payments to a great extent.

Despite the opportunities that lie ahead, it is important to reconsider that growth in mobile payments in the US substantially lags some other mature, large-scale economies such as China. The use of mobile payments by US consumers has been lackluster at best. The lag is very surprising given the rates of adoption and usage of mobile banking.

However, over the next three years mobile payments will see strong growth in the US too. Consumers will become more adoptive of the technology and payments providers will do a far better job of enhancing and marketing mobile payment services.

Additionally, a real dichotomy exists in the US contactless payments landscape where, according to data provided by Visa, in 2018 just 5 percent of cards issued had contactless capability (7 percent of credit cards and 1 percent of debit cards). The upside potential is huge as, in March 2020, 71 percent of face-to-face transactions in the US occurred at contactless enabled locations.

Meanwhile—just like the mobile payments story—other countries have seen tremendous growth in contactless payments:

- Australia is one of the leading contactless payments markets in the world. In 2018, Visa reported that 92 percent of face-to-face Visa transactions used a contactless payment method.
- In Brazil, 70 percent of retail point-of-sale terminals accept contactless payments and a surge in transactions is expected to follow.
- Canada is also way ahead, with more than fifty contactless transactions per second being processed.
- In Hong Kong, contactless face-to-face Visa transactions have surged to one-in-three transactions.
- In the UK, contactless payment transactions increased by more than 90 percent last year, and Transport for London (TfL)—which accounts for most transit transactions—has processed more than a billion contactless payment journeys since launch in September 2014.

MOBILE COMMUNICATIONS GET SMARTER

The jump from 3G to 4G brought with it the revolutionary era of smartphones, mobile banking and e-commerce. To provide some perspective, 5G will be 100 times faster than 4G, and 10 times faster than your average broadband connection today (Sievewright, 5G - What Will I.T. Mean?, 2019). In other words, imagine downloading a movie on your smartphone in a matter of seconds.

With one to ten gigabits connection speeds, 5G is at the core of powering autonomous vehicles, smart factories (what is being called industrial IoT), remotely controlled drones, virtual reality, augmented reality and mixed reality devices, in-home IoT, and the world's first smart cities. 5G is about to allow every person on earth to tap into data from billions of sensors around the globe. It is the promise of on-demand knowledge for anyone, anywhere, anytime.

5G will facilitate a world of trillions of sensors and devices. As the global population of online users doubles, modern society is about to experience perhaps the most historic acceleration of progress and technological innovation in history.

Payments from mobile devices and wearables may be enhanced by 5G for both the merchant and the consumer. The benefits of accelerated payment authentication and proactive fraud detection could also be wins for routine point-of-sale transactions.

The increase in speed and reduction in latency could allow margin for additional processes to be inserted that help reduce fraud detection errors. Consumers could more confidently use their preferred method of payment, enjoying faster transactions and personalized services without fearing unnecessary payment locks.

Mobile payments made by 5G-connected devices could be more securely authorized by what appears to be an instant cross-reference of merchant ID, transaction amount, geolocation and biometrics. Personal budgeting apps could also provide near-immediate feedback about a purchase and its budget implications by rapidly importing transaction data.

5G can enable financial institutions to extend their reach by providing a complete branch experience at temporary locations like sporting events, concerts, college campuses, and disaster-affected areas. The speed and responsiveness of 5G could enable simultaneous wireless functionality of ATM and other self-service kiosks, employee telepresence, teller systems, Wi-Fi, and video surveillance, as well as entertainment and digital signage for lounge areas.

5G is expected to remove performance issues with payments made via wearables and IoT connected devices. Equally important will be all the enhancements that 5G brings to other transactions made with a mobile device.

For example, because 5G allows more data to travel across networks in real-time, it will enhance proactive fraud prevention. As soon as a consumer initiates a mobile payment transaction, financial institutions will be able to rapidly comb through data like geolocation, transaction amounts, and merchant IDs to reduce fraud detection errors. As a result, fewer legitimate mobile transactions will be wrongly declined at the point of sale for (incorrectly) suspected fraud.

By leveraging the speed and capacity in this new wireless world, financial institutions that invest in tools to combine artificial intelligence, data, and 5G will be able to run many parallel processes in real time. In turn, it could improve the speed and accuracy behind lending decisions and will optimize lending rates to match each unique applicant's reality. And thanks to 5G's high-resolution streaming capabilities, consumers will have real-time access to video consultations with financial experts (human and digital) who can help them make informed financing decisions.

The advent of 5G is set to be a revolutionary moment in the development of mobile internet connectivity. As 5G networks come online, they will bring with them the promise of unprecedented speed, low latency, and the capacity to carry huge numbers of connections simultaneously. The arrival of 5G will allow financial institutions to launch new products and services not previously possible, move into new markets and increase productivity.

Unlike 4G and LTE connections, the use cases of 5G will not be limited merely to mobile phones; it will be transformative in many other ways. With sensors being placed in everything from mobile phones and household appliances to cars and lamp posts, 5G will power the internet of things and provide the infrastructure to carry huge amounts of data, allowing for a smarter and more connected world.

Familiar banking operations such as payment services will attain new forms extending to newer channels, including 5G smartphones, wearables, IOT devices and virtual reality. Wearables are already becoming an important channel for mobile payments, and this is likely to increase as 5G becomes available.

The proliferation of 5G networks is also likely to have a significant impact on fintech, itself a great disruptor of the financial services industry. Some fintechs may have first-mover advantage as early adoption of 5G may be one way for them to increase further their market share, win more customers and drive value creation.

5G will require credit unions to significantly rethink the ways they use technology for internal operations and member (customer) engagement alike. It is time to get ready!

A WHOLE NEW WORLD OF PAYMENTS

The US payments system is undergoing rapid (arguably, unprecedented) change as innovation, technology advances, consumer preferences, and increased competition continue to redefine this highly valuable and lucrative aspect of the financial services business. "Financial institutions will need to devise focused payments-related strategies that can respond to the changing needs and demands of their consumers as well as keep pace with new solutions and technologies that are reshaping the consumer experience" (Sievewright, Perspectives Report: The Future of Payments, 2018).

Developing and executing a successful payments strategy will bring obvious financial benefits. Also, financial institutions should be mindful of the fact that payments will provide access to transaction data and insights. Rich perceptions about the context of each payment transaction can prove invaluable in deepening the financial relationship and delivering an outstanding service experience.

REFERENCES

GovMint.com, a brand of Asset Marketing Services, LLC. (n.d.). *Ancient Coins*. Retrieved from GovMint.com: https://www.govmint.com/other/ancient-coins

Sievewright, M. (2018). *Perspectives Report: The Future of Payments*. Sievewright & Associates.

Sievewright, M. (2019). *5G - What Will I.T. Mean?* Sievewright & Associates.

Statista. (2020). *Digital Payments*. Retrieved from statista: https://www.statista.com/statistics/763617/venmo-total-payment-volume/

The Federal Reserve. (2017, September 6). *Strategies for Improving the US Payment System*. Retrieved from https://www.federalreserve.gov/newsevents/pressreleases/files/other20170906a1.pdf

The Federal Reserve. (2019). *The 2019 Federal Reserve Payments Study*. Retrieved from Board of Governors of the Fed-

eral Reserve System: https://www.federalreserve.gov/
paymentsystems/2019-December-The-Federal-Reserve-
Payments-Study.htm

9.
UBER PERSONALIZATION

A GLIMPSE OF THE FUTURE

MIDWAY INTO THE TWENTIETH CENTURY, right at the dawn of digital automation, financial and personal data had to be transcribed from paper forms into computer-readable media. Almost forgotten, old computer media included punched cards, punched tape, and magnetic tape.

The data entry process was painstakingly slow, as physical forms and media had to be shuttled to the respective processing sites. The bulk of information fed to the computer would then be processed overnight as sluggish batches of data. As the saying goes, *hindsight is 20/20*, so these stark limitations of batch data processing are most apparent from the vantage point of the digital decade of 2020.

As automation has accelerated through successive waves of innovation, it is best to fast forward into the tantalizing digital realities and upcoming novelties of the 2020s. Online interactions generate a wealth of customer data, usually produced through endless on-screen clicks and typing.

The digital age will greatly expand the quantity, richness, and intimacy of customer information that enterprises may obtain dynamically in real time. Such live digital feedback loops are likely to augment the data from customer signals by at least two orders of magnitude, or in lay terms, more than 100 times. Could people manage to click and type at such a fast pace?

As it turns out, smartphones and other personal digital devices can automatically capture massive amounts of live customer-related data. For example, mobile devices may clearly pinpoint their actual location. Cameras and digital sensors connected to artificial intelligence engines may estimate the age and sense the mood of the bearer.

Additionally, personal apps would gain intimate insights about the agenda, friends, and whereabouts of the user. Every click counts, resulting in a rich stream of telemetry that gives app providers deep insights about each customer. Whereas ethical commercial practices and regulations are giving customers some degree of control over their privacy, many people would willfully choose to opt in or accept sharing some basic information in return for using the apps.

Digital device types go well beyond personal computers, laptops, tablets, or smartphones. Take gaming consoles with multiplayer games. These interactions may reflect the behavioral patterns of a gamer within a team or under pressure. And personal health monitoring wristbands contain sensors that can capture heartrates and other personal vital indicators.

Individuals may also connect their medical devices for monitoring and tracking special conditions. Or the most recent expressions of mixed reality headsets can allow a person to interact with a combination of real world and digital holograms.

The depth and breadth of the aggregate personal information coming from all the digital interactions, transactions, and real-time feedback loops from apps and devices plus the digital insights that are collected about an individual at every point of interaction builds up to brutal personal knowledge! For most people, these personal digital insights would largely exceed their own self-awareness capabilities.

Figure 15 – Digital precision in personal knowledge

Mixed reality, combined with artificial intelligence, has enormous potential to augment the level of understanding about the interactions of a person with their surroundings. Machine learning algorithms can learn about the individual interaction patterns and recommend effective actions in real-time.

Cognitive services can help visualize, classify, cluster, and interpret images interactively and with utmost accuracy. For example, in professions such as healthcare workers or high-stakes traders, specialized knowledge must be applied live in mission-critical tasks. Here, personalized artificial intelligence would augment the capabilities of an individual and increase the level of talent across the workforce.

SOFTWARE SOLUTIONS FOR EVERY PERSON?

Digital devices are becoming a natural extension of the individual. For many years, people have grown accustomed to the speed of air travel and the convenience of the automobile. Much in the same way that modern transportation has greatly shrank physical distances for humans, intelligent personal devices will significantly expand the reach, ability, and depth of understanding of every individual.

These devices stoke an even faster growth in the already mushrooming amounts of unstructured and structured data attached to digital media and social network activities. And the ubiquitous cloud is now powering a wide range of software for innovative personal services.

Cloud technologies are accelerating the software development cycle and therefore giving rise to very rapid, inexpensive custom solutions. Agile development methodologies build on continuous integration and continuous delivery capabilities that enable the rapid deployment of successive chunks of application software functionality.

Enterprises may then deliver innovative custom features, practically on the spot, to meet and shape up the continually fluctuating needs of their increasingly granular customer segments. For example, Microsoft's serverless computing known as Azure Functions (Microsoft Corporation, 2019), enable clients to easily develop and run small pieces of software code, or functions, to tackle the challenge at hand without worrying about a whole application or the infrastructure to run it.

Software development is supporting a new age of digital agility. Large, multi-year development projects to orchestrate complex, one-size-fits-all, collective enterprise-grade functionalities are giving way to more discrete projects. Hence the opportunity to customize features and functions at a much more granular level.

For complex developments, cross-functional project management techniques facilitate a comprehensive scope with rich, inclusive functions. In contrast, agile methodologies provide for an iterative and collaborative development approach with continuous integration of smaller chunks of work (also known as sprints).

Such discrete development chunks enable ultra-fine customization and continuous delivery of new features, almost daily. Rapid and continual experimentation by a very large number of digital users provides immediate feedback. Software solutions would be adjusted dynamically based on the success of new features and functions as well as fresh ideas and opportunities for improvement.

Contributions from and to the open source community can greatly amplify the richness and value of these custom developments. As the delivery and customer feedback cycle shortens so significantly, institutions can fast-track innovations that get personalized to meet the changing preferences of virtually every individual.

TECHNOLOGY GETS PERSONAL

Pervasive cloud processing and intelligent digital devices are taking part of everyday life. Personal parameters, such as biometrics and location provide a rich context to inform live digital interactions and strengthen information security.

For example, smartphones can authenticate their bearers through facial recognition algorithms. And video monitoring cameras operating remotely may use similar artificial intelligence capabilities to detect unusual activity. Much in the way that personal digital agents can help with everyday tasks, individuals can control their own private artificial intelligence features.

Optical character recognition, coupled with natural language understanding, serve as another example of intelligent personal interaction features that augment individual intelligence and productivity. And a variety of sensors on wearable devices can instantly update the bearer on indicators, such as personal vitals, and alert on the surroundings.

Intelligent cognitive services can amplify perception and narrate what a smartphone camera sees or, like GPS navigation apps, use audible beacons to guide an individual through a path to reach a destination. What value will these personal signals bring?

The universe of instant digital interactions will create billions of instant segments of one. Cloud processing can scale efficiently to process such multitude of personal digital signals in real-time. Such an ultra-fine level of analytics would empower both digital service providers and people to get personalized insights at the point of decision, even to inform everyday activities.

For instance, artificial intelligence allows the mining of millions of real-life situations to model next-best-action and next-best-offer hypotheses to suit the instant needs and preferences of an individual accurately and effectively. And the granularity of personal-level analytics will thrive on individual mood, behavioral traits, social media, and situational context. Can these analytics surpass the insights that people have on their own?

WHERE DIGITAL ANALYTICS MEET HUMAN REALITIES

In principle, the human mind has deep capabilities, such as common sense and intuition, that still prove quite difficult to model. Therefore, digital intelligence merely makes a lame attempt to represent and act upon a continually changing gamut of individual beliefs, cultures, values, and on-the-spot preferences.

On the other hand, massive and repetitive interactions such as millions of individuals typing a query or browsing smartphone screens serve as very useful fodder for artificial intelligence algorithms. To the point that just the first keystroke on a query can instantly populate a small set of very accurate suggestions to effectively complete the search argument.

Contextual parameters such as detailed activity records of individual interactions, locations, gestures, and time, all aggregated at a global scale, will greatly augment the predictive power and accuracy of such well-informed guesses. Could such aggregate digital intelligence fare better than humans?

Perhaps the short-term answer lies in examples of what may go wrong, for example, cybersecurity issues. Unfortunately, personal information might be exploited for criminal, unethical, or damaging purposes, or erroneous, fake, or plainly false statements about otherwise rightful facts or persons.

It is the same when something goes wrong, as human nature tends to seek an apparent cause, entity, or person to blame for the mishap. Uncontrolled, pernicious digital virality may readily exploit collective beliefs or bias, as well as individual emotions, naivete, predisposition, or sheer gullibility.

The ensuing exposure to collective, rush-to-judgment virality may escalate out of proportion instantly and without control, and end up producing severe harm to legitimat causes, enterprises, or individuals.

Beware of any *digital truth* that spreads virally. People may take it at face value and without any further analysis, evidence, explanation, rationale, or substance. Absent fundamental drivers such as common sense and ethical principles, blatant lies might ride instant digital amplification to override facts and damage reputations. Can humans control such a swarm of digital negativities?

SENSIBLE DIGITAL PROTECTIONS OR CENSORSHIP?

Artificial intelligence is becoming essential to ensure enterprise and individual safety (and health) in the digital world. For instance, it can effectively be used to curtail malware and virus attacks or to issue timely warnings and provide immediate mitigating responses to fend off cybersecurity threats.

Along these lines, pernicious virality could use *circuit-breakers* that may apply some form of digital common sense, while still honoring free speech principles. Sensible and ethical digital logic could detect, and slow down or stop, tempests of disinformation that ride on social media and similar instant dissemination mechanisms before the damage becomes dire.

For common sense to prevail, sane minds should be able to quickly overcome the freewheeling plethora of digital stimuli coming from collective sources and personal devices. Well-known statistical tools, such as personal filters and reasonability tests may help. Ditto with machine-learning gimmicks such as anomaly detection.

However, these digital tools may still fall short of understanding the meaning of unexpected viral trends in a snap. Systemic accountability, personal and privacy filters, together with the ability to transparently explain the context and credibility of the facts and sources, may effectively augment human defenses against harmful virality. At the end of the day, individuals may pull such sound personalized digital advice and controls to better balance their reaction.

COLLAPSING THE PERCEPTION OF TIME AND SPACE

On the positive side, deep insights about personal preferences can reveal unmet, unarticulated needs. Providers may then instantly customize product and service features that may wow virtually everyone, every time.

A largely untapped field of opportunity for financial institutions rests in combining personalized financial products and services with commerce and lifestyle needs. For instance, mixed reality technologies like Microsoft HoloLens enable individuals to interactively explore their financial capacity while picturing themselves at the car, home, college, or vacation of their dreams.

A myriad digital stimuli is activating some surprising behaviors in the human brain, a prime example being an innate ability to multitask seamlessly among rapid bursts of concurrent threads. These abilities are becoming more prominent in the born digital generations, and the constant quest for instant response to fleeting text, acoustic, and visual stimuli may result in a visible reduction of the attention span.

What are the typical signs of such emerging digital psyche? Perhaps a continual impulse to seek new forms of digital pleasure that rides on superficial and short-lived thrills. Or the need to stay connected all the time to the point of subordinating physical activities to digital interactions (hence the advice: *do not text and drive*).

By analogy to the theory of special relativity, the perception of time may elapse differently depending on the digital speed of each individual psyche. To grasp how this subjective time clock operates, suffice it to say that it seems to tick faster under sudden stress. In the physical world, people may recall such subjective time warps when they survive a traumatic moving accident.

Under stress, time seems to run more slowly. And multiple spaces seem to collapse into flashes of manifold images. Therefore, the relentless stress attached to successive spikes of digital stimuli may affect the individual perception of time and space, thus numbing the sensitivity to the actual dimensions and pace of real life.

How can a healthy brain adapt to this frantic digital velocity and reconcile with the real world? Perhaps the answer may stem from the ability of the brain to efficiently attach a split-second timestamp to diverse digital and physical stimuli that could help in adequately internalizing, reconciling, and sequencing the perception of digital and physical events.

Whether they manifest through virality or behavioral changes, pervasive digital deeds can cause unforeseen, long-term consequences. Among other perils, digital activities may distort the perceived value of physical work and the need to produce goods and services, particularly as automation and robotics change the industrial production paradigm.

Like the fable of the lazy grasshopper and the ant that labors tirelessly to stock food to survive the winter, digital pathologies may deride and eschew the effort to produce and fulfill more basic needs. The typical personalities of digital geeks that may seem impervious to physical appearances and similarly, the cases of digitally spoiled brats who may attack viciously any fact or opinion that crosses their path and disregard human advice are good examples.

THE QUEST FOR PERSONAL MEANING

Language diversity presents another interesting twist in the advent of intelligent digital interactions. Over many centuries, an ease of travel coupled with economic power has been favoring the adoption of widely accepted, common business languages. Many migrants saw their descendants naturally adopt, and assimilate to, the language (and customs) of their host country.

Artificial intelligence is providing real-time, universal speech and text translation for an increasingly vast array of international languages (and dialects). Therefore, digital translation now makes it easier to preserve the native language of an individual and empower people globally to overcome language barriers and communicate fluently in their own tongue.

A highly connected digital lifestyle may raise the individual awareness of social issues, and possibly exacerbate their significance. On a positive note, active participation in social networks may result in the digital fulfillment of top level human needs for belongingness (and influence) within Maslow's hierarchy (Maslow, 1943).

A surge of digital activism in social media however, as opposed to direct person-to-person exchange and influence, could cause unintended consequences. One radical opinion might stir collective swings in public opinion and affect properly established trust in institutions or people.

For many organizations, the ability and willingness to harness digital interactions to the benefit of each person will become a fundamental challenge. Granting customers and employees ample access to the digital world can stimulate individual curiosity and a passion to advance personal progress.

Thanks to modern and more dynamic collaboration schema, the digital workplace can break down (individual) communication barriers. Organizations can attract scarcely available new talent by offering the progressive and innovative environments that top candidates now expect.

Notwithstanding the imperatives to duly protect confidential and private information, organizations should also cater to such constructive purposes of digital information sharing. How can institutions ensure authenticity?

Personal identity constitutes another struggle between the physical and digital worlds. Which one would be more reliable and trustworthy, if not absolute? Can people trust digital records blindly, and disregard physical evidence? In the digital world, fraudulent impersonation of individuals can be most damaging, as identity theft may wreak havoc with personal finances and credit worthiness.

The legal standing of digital transaction records is also at issue. Institutions need to properly protect these records from unauthorized alteration and preserve an immutable audit trail of all (properly availed) modifications. An increased emphasis on data privacy principles and regulations is granting better controls to individuals of their personal information that gets shared digitally, and empowering people to expect some tangible value in return.

Equipping mobile devices with facial recognition biometrics can add a necessary level of protection. For example, Apple Inc. has built on biometric authentication to coin a most telling phrase: what happens on the iPhone stays on the iPhone (iphonefirmware.com, 2019).

FULFILLING INDIVIDUAL NEEDS

To understand the unarticulated needs of their customers or prospects, institutions must find a way to understand the complete personal situation of each individual. For starters, financial institutions host a wealth of basic customer and transactional data that resides in their core systems.

For each customer, institutions have a rich history of financial records, to include deposits, investments, withdrawals, and payments. In addition, institutions derive insightful indicators of individual financial performance when doing the risk analysis to extend diverse types of credit facilities. This is valuable data, but is that all?

Personal interactions, stemming from conversations with account executives, tellers, and client service personnel may further enrich the wealth of financial data with deep insights about life events or customer situations. Furthermore, individual interactions through mobile and online banking channels may add non-financial intelligence about the patterns of behavior and preferences of a given customer. Besides all this wealth of internal customer information, customers continually have many more external digital lifestyle interactions in the external world that financial institutions may need to add.

Strategic alliances between financial institutions and partnerships with a vibrant ecosystem of digital service providers will be pivotal to complete the picture of individual needs, for example, with retailers that gain direct insights about individual shopping behaviors and habits.

Also, the stream of millions of signals that arrive from the digital feedback loop that spans a rising cadre of intelligent personal devices and sensors, also known as the intelligent edge. Powerful machine-learning algorithms can harvest this aggregate and vast wealth of financial and non-financial data to make accurate predictions at the individual level.

Imagine a world where you could predict when your members will have their first thought about retirement planning and be ready to help them create that plan in just minutes. Imagine you could do the same for a family planning to apply for their mortgage or a start-up small business deciding where to bank for the first time. Now imagine you can address each of these situations for members wherever they are, anytime, on any device and without any rising costs.

Credit unions and banks have more data on their members/customers than anyone else. But they still struggle to extract meaningful information and use it for good business decisions. Data is key to the transformation of financial services. The amount of structured and unstructured data that financial institutions need to analyze has grown—and will continue to grow—exponentially. The now frequently heard metaphor that *Data is the new oil* acknowledges the important role of data to fuel future advances and innovation. If data is indeed the new oil, then advanced analytic technologies are the way to refine it (Sievewright, 2019).

Extremely rich customer data, combined with advanced machine-learning algorithms, and now riding on the mighty computing power of the public cloud, can swiftly attain utmost accurate predictions practically at the individual level. Still, it is all about feeding data to the computer in a format and manner that computers may digest.

Advanced machine learning can glean very insightful patterns and trends from this data, as well as classify and cluster individual behaviors and facts much faster than humans. And even pick up subtleties that escape the human grasp. A nagging question however, hinges on how well computers may understand human emotions. Could computers act with empathy?

INDIVIDUAL DIGITAL INTENSITY

Given the heightened concerns about climate change, it may be worth analyzing some projections about how individuals will consume energy in thirty years. *Exhibit 23* compares the residential energy consumption per person in 2018 and the projections for 2050, across selected countries.

Whereas individual energy consumption in countries outside the Organization for Economic Co-operation and Development (OECD) is expected to grow at a steady clip of 1.32 percent annually, it will contract in OECD countries (U.S. Energy Information Administration, 2019). Among other potential future changes, these estimates acknowledge the uncertainty attached to future technological breakthroughs and energy related regulations.

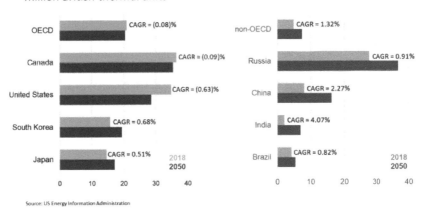

Residential energy consumption per person (2018–2050)
million British thermal units

Source: US Energy Information Administration

Exhibit 23 – Residential energy consumption (2018–2050)

What revealing factors will be driving such diverging growth rates? As global economic growth would bridge the gap in income inequality and lagging infrastructure in large countries such as India and China, the access to residential energy will spark average individual consumption. For these two countries, the respective compound annual growth rates (CAGR) are estimated at 4.07 percent and 2.27 percent respectively. Such growth stands out starkly when compared to Japan, South Korea, and the overall contraction in OECD countries. What else would then influence individual energy consumption by country?

A relentless drop in the total world population growth rate represents another influencing factor. As depicted in *Exhibit 24*, the world population growth rate has been declining noticeably since 1965 (The World Bank, 2019). Such decline in growth rates is much less pronounced in most African and Middle Eastern countries, where the population continued to grow at rates between 1.5 percent and 3.5 percent in 2018. For most developed countries, an already low and declining trend in population growth rates would imply a lower demand for energy consumption by household.

Despite the generalized decline in growth rates, the total world population has already surpassed the 7.6 billion mark in 2020 (United States Census Bureau, 2020). Improvements in living standards across the world also entail an increasing demand for energy, to produce goods and services for individual consumption. And all over the world, industrial uses will continue to increase their demand for energy.

Increasing demand will also stem from a significant, albeit often overlooked factor: the digital intensity consumed by every individual. Besides the already significant demand for energy by vehicles, household appliances, air conditioning, and heating, an array of entertainment, gaming, household robots, internet of things, and personal digital devices will require much more energy than lightbulbs, hence the marginal impact of daylight savings time!

For most developed countries, would such increase in individual digital intensity tend to offset the continuing decline in population growth and overall energy efficiency of industrial and household consumption?

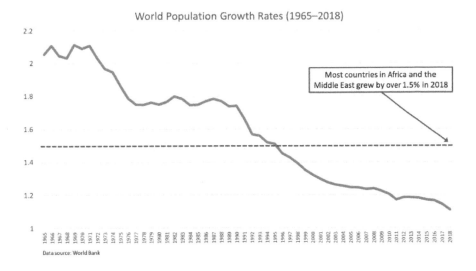

Exhibit 24 – World population growth rates (1965–2018)

While many organizations strive to prove or disprove models and theories about the plausible impact of carbon emission, reduction, and removal on planet Earth, humanity will continue to consume more energy. Notwithstanding the policies and politics around this theme, most companies and individuals are becoming increasingly savvy about energy efficiency and carbon content. How will personal choice help in curbing energy consumption?

Choosing to drive an electric car or ride sharing, plus the development of comfortable and reliable mass transportation systems, and most importantly, employing intelligent systems that optimize energy utilization at home and at work are key. Whereas such intelligent systems and individual digital intensity will intrinsically consume more energy, the result will be smarter consumption, and therefore, more efficiency overall.

What will be the impact of digital intensity at a personal level? It will hinge on adaptive intelligent lifestyle systems that give individuals a greater ability to choose, in a dynamic and interactive manner. Such instant adaptability and dynamic choice will become a quintessential pillar of uber personalization.

Another key pillar will be the intelligence to advise, and ultimately guide, an individual through optimally personalized choices. For example, in the case of energy consumption, a personal agent may pop up relevant insights at every instant about the individual's whereabouts and recommend practical options and steps to optimize the use of energy.

In a futuristic scenario, intelligent agents will learn from the continual choices, habits, and preferences of a person. Such intimate personal knowledge will give rise to a powerful breed of individual predictive apps. Well beyond the personal financial information held in a bank, credit union, or brokerage account, these intelligent agents will hold very granular, instant-by-instant details about the individual choices and actions. And they will help every person formulate and manage their lifestyle goals and behaviors.

PERSONAL DIGITAL HEALTH AND LIFE BALANCE

Wearable tracking devices have been trending in the popular terrain of managing individual health and well-being and serve as a practical example of what intelligent agents can achieve in the real-time, uber personalization domain. Going forward, these health apps may incorporate feeds from diverse vital signs, health records, and environmental parameters. Riding on such predictive power and timely advice, for example, a person may end up catching a common cold only if he or she wanted to!

Cognitive services, such as facial recognition, can also detect the mood of an individual by analyzing typical expressions. Similarly, voice recognition systems can gage individual emotions through the pitch and tone, and even detect variations in the words that a person chooses or how they articulate usual sentences. By distinguishing instant signs of anger, distress, and pain from those related to happiness and positive surprise, individual health agents can help people sort out situations quickly and take immediate action to mitigate any trouble or extend a healthy opportunity.

Besides lowering the energy consumption and healthcare bills of an individual, intelligent health apps will give valuable personalized advice on how to live a better (and longer) life, like how to get a most restful and repairing good night's sleep.

In the financial domain, healthier living will consequently help in lowering individual insurance premiums, and possibly, credit interest rates. In any case, most people will significantly appreciate the contribution that digital health may bring to their quality of life.

Similarly, individual intelligent apps could advise on how to strike an optimal balance between financials, lifestyle, and spending. Obviously, such apps will need to allay any privacy concerns and combine a wealth of data about the individual borrowing, saving, investing, and payments habits, with very fine information about the person's personal lifestyle and health habits.

Financial institutions may therefore find interesting opportunities to insert themselves in this uber personalization and life purpose. When tapped in concert with an ecosystem of digital providers, such opportunities will add new dimensions of trust and value to the individual financial relationships.

REFERENCES

iphonefirmware.com. (2019, January). *Ahead of CES, Apple touts 'what happens on your iPhone, stays on your iPhone' with privacy billboard in Las Vegas.* Retrieved from iphonefirmware.com: https://www.iphonefirmware.com/ahead-of-ces-apple-touts-what-happens-on-your-iphone-stays-on-your-iphone-with-privacy-billboard-in-las-vegas/

Maslow, A. (1943). A Theory of Human Motivation. *Psychological Review, American Psychological Association.*

Microsoft Corporation. (2019). *An Introduction to Azure Functions.* Retrieved from Microsoft Azure: https://docs.microsoft.com/en-us/azure/azure-functions/functions-overview

Sievewright, M. (2019, February). *The Age of Data Analytics.* Retrieved from Perspectives Report: www.sievewrightandassociates.com

The World Bank. (2019, December 20). *Population Growth Annual % - World Development Indicators.* Retrieved from DataBank: https://data.worldbank.org/indicator/sp.pop.grow

US Energy Information Administration. (2019, September). *International Energy Outlook 2019.* Retrieved from US Energy Information Administration: https://www.eia.gov/outlooks/ieo/

United States Census Bureau. (2020). *US and World Population Clock.* Retrieved from United States Census Bureau: https://www.census.gov/popclock/

10.
DIGITAL IDENTITY AND PRIVACY

THE DIGITAL SCOURGE OF IDENTITY THEFT

WOULD THE PUBLIC CLOUD BE good or bad news for financial services? Would it end up compromising the fiduciary responsibility to protect customer data, confidentiality, and privacy? Many executives at traditional institutions, feeling besieged by continual waves of digital innovation, wonder about this issue.

Could the thriving public cloud, like other dazzling new technologies turn out to be harmful? Any which way and well before the arrival of the cloud, institutions had become dependent on another shared digital service: the electronic communications networks.

Like many other innovations, the public cloud together with its interconnected digital services, are meant to serve legitimate economic and social purposes. However, these innovations might be wrongly put to criminal or damaging uses which negate their intended constructive purpose. This paradigm between peaceful or violent use is nothing new.

Perhaps a most telling case goes back to the invention of dynamite by Alfred Nobel in 1867 (Britannica, 1995). Whereas dynamite was originally conceived for the safer use of explosives in mining and construction, it was also repurposed as a weapon. To leave a positive legacy, Nobel donated a good part of his wealth accrued from armament and other factories to institute the annual Nobel Prize awards in sciences, literature, and peace.

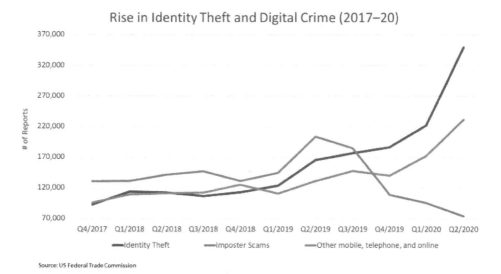

Exhibit 25 – Rise in identity theft and digital crime (2017–2020)

And financial services executives have every reason to be concerned about the misuse of online technologies. The digital age has spawned a plethora of fraudulent scams and crimes. Global online access is exacerbating the threat. Whereas not all incidents get reported, *Exhibit 25* highlights how much identity theft cases spiked in 2019.

Other significant imposter scams, also tracked by the FTC Consumer Sentinel Network (US Federal Trade Commission, 2019), entail fraudsters posing primarily as government agents, technology support services, or bogus business representatives. Reports on various mobile, telephone, and online crimes are also trending upwards.

DIGITAL ISOLATION?

Cutting off all communications and touch points with the outside world could well serve as a plausible initial defense against a pernicious and unknown attacker. To shield against any accidental or intentional intrusion, the perimeter of the individual location could be fortified. And the location could be locked out to stop and prevent any movement or transport coming from outside.

As an additional preventative action, just in case a single stray intruder had made it inside, the entire location could be subject to a deep cleansing that would wipe out practically all extraneous intruder holdouts, no matter how tiny. And healthy, trusted countermeasures could further reinforce existing defenses.

Then, to round up such initial defense, a strident and almost deafening alarm would go off whenever there was an indication that the intruder may still be on site. Just in case, the entire location would set in motion all possible protective measures.

Does this scenario sound like an individual defense against a wanton cyberattack or an epidemic breakout? It might well be any of the two. The point is that in the digital age, many people are becoming paranoid about their privacy.

Cybercrime and outright misuse of personal information can wreak havoc in the digital, financial, and social health of any individual. Then, it is understandable that a person's immediate reaction would be to cut off the flow of information and get isolated from the digital world.

What would be the trade-offs and long-term consequences of digital isolation? In principle, individuals would be unable to access a wealth of innovative digital services that keep cropping up continually all over the world. Absolute digital isolation would also carry lasting negative financial and social repercussions.

In today's world, doing business in person, on paper, is an increasingly cumbersome option that many entities may no longer support. And those who still accept such manual transactions are ultimately posting them to their core systems and working with the corresponding digital records. As indirect digitalization seems inevitable, individuals would have a hard time enforcing their self-proclaimed isolation. They will also have to endure the parochial alienation that paper transactions bring.

Somebody may come up with a wondrous idea to outlaw all viruses and their carriers. In the case of highly contagious microbial infections, such a move would prove ineffective. For computer viruses, an equivalent move might add just a bit of deterrence to the sources that develop such malicious software. What about privacy? Could regulations boost privacy defenses by restricting the behaviors of potential sources of privacy breaches?

THE RIGHT TO DIGITAL PRIVACY AND SOVEREIGNTY

Beyond the zeal from financial institutions to safeguard the data that individuals or companies entrust to them, several government bodies are passing legislation to protect any personal information that gets stored or transmitted electronically. Besides its significance as a regulatory requirement, many companies see privacy as a fundamental human right that must be protected (Smith, 2019).

Given the global nature of the internet and public cloud services, contentious litigation may arise when government agencies seek to access personal and private information that companies may be hosting across jurisdictions. As cybercrime also affects today's digitally interconnected world, all domestic networks are nevertheless exposed to attacks from foreign actors.

In 2016, the European Union adopted the General Data Protection Regulation (GDPR) that aims to give greater control to individuals over their personal data. Among other requirements, it mandates companies to heed the right of consumers to change or delete their information, which company systems may be storing, and notify them promptly when their information gets compromised. Countries such as Australia and Brazil have adopted similar privacy requirements to those in GDPR.

In the US, the California Consumer Privacy Act (CCPA) enforced in 2020 (State of California Department of Justice, 2018) established new rights to California consumers, namely:

- The right to know what personal information is collected, used, shared, or sold
- The right to delete personal information held by businesses
- The right to opt out of the sale of personal information
- The right to non-discrimination in terms of price or service when a consumer exercises a privacy right under CCPA

For most financial institutions, complying with such privacy regulations requires a significant overhaul of many of their existing technology systems and operating procedures. Individuals leave their digital fingerprints as they operate electronic devices, namely, the internet IP address of their device, the location of their smartphone, their log-in activity, or their connection to a Wi-Fi network. Fortunately, many technology providers, to include public cloud services, have taken decisive and effective steps to help institutions accelerate compliance.

THREATS WITHOUT BORDERS

Will privacy regulations end up protecting citizens or criminals? Cyberattacks that capture personal data for fraudulent use continue to rise. These threats include a potentially devastating impact whenever nation-state hacking groups orchestrate cyberattacks.

The prospects of cyberwarfare will complicate matters further, as rivaling countries develop sophisticated software weapons and defenses and may enact extreme measures in case of conflict. It may then be argued that granting criminals the same rights to privacy would hamper proper action by law enforcement agencies.

Fortunately, the law is catching up with cyberthreats and digital crime. In the US, the Clarifying Lawful Overseas Use of Data Act (CLOUD Act) was passed along with the provisions on Law Enforcement within the Consolidated Appropriations Act of 2018.

This CLOUD Act seeks to resolve situations where companies hold personal information, and are therefore bound by privacy regulations, may face conflicting laws between sovereign jurisdictions. In particular, US authorities may use warrants and subpoenas to require service providers based in the US to furnish the requested data regardless of whether the data repository is located within the US or abroad (Wikipedia, n.d.).

Isolated actions, such as the futile attempts to isolate company computer systems from the outside world will prove ineffective. Indeed, the advanced information protection features would surpass the level of security that can be attained by a bank, credit union, securities firm, or insurance company. Financial institutions will need to partner and work together with their respective authorities in multilateral efforts to curtail cyberattacks, particularly those organized by international actors.

PERSONAL IDENTITY

How can institutions ascertain and confirm the identity of an individual? Before the digital age, personal rapport and side-by-side signature verification, by trained branch personnel, of an original on (paper) file was deemed to be enough. The digital age has changed the burden of identity verification dramatically, particularly for remote access, to involve a combination of multiple authentication factors such as:

- Personal user identification (for online access)
- User password (strong combination)
- One-time password (to approve a transaction or reset a password)
- Personal identification number (PIN)
- Authentication code (obtained by phone, electronically, or cryptographically)
- Personal information (e.g., address, phone number, names, date of birth, gender)
- Account number
- Bank card data (e.g., number, expiration date, verification code)
- Documentation (e.g., driver license, national ID, passport, credential)
- Personal signature (digitalized or physical)
- Photo identification on file (digitalized)
- Physical location and whereabouts of the individual (e.g., smartphone location)
- Entitlements (e.g., access permissions, authorized hours)
- Physical or digital authentication token (in the person's possession)
- Certificate (digital or physical, issued by a trusted authority)
- Direct attestation (by a company or government authority)

- Biometrics (fingerprints, facial traits, voice, mood)
- Behavioral biometrics (how the individual interacts with an application or device)
- Digital identification of the device (e.g., IP address, browser cookies)
- Answers to personalized challenges (e.g., friends, schools, lifestyle events)

Given the rising threat of identity theft and regulations requiring more robust authentication, financial institutions watch for warning signs or indications that a pattern of attacks is taking place. For example, before authenticating a caller and discussing account information or transactions, contact center personnel may trigger a series of deeper authentication probes. Like the tedious chorus line in the song by The Beatles entitled *Revolution 9* (Lennon-McCartney, 1968), such repetitive questioning procedure may end up lacking practical meaning: *number 9, number 9, number 9...*

On one hand, additional and detailed questions could strengthen the identity verification. However, excess and intrusive questions may undermine productivity and irritate genuine clients, customers, or members. What would be the right balance between reassurances and service? Could the computer records of an institution carry inaccurate or false information and cause an authentication exception?

Given a greater reliance on a multitude of digital records and authentication factors, institutions tend to trust their own information, to the point that when these records get altered by an impostor, the institution might doubt the rightful accountholder even when they show up in person holding a valid identification. Should such a situation call for investigating a possible incident of identity theft? Could individuals gain better control over their identity?

COMPROMISE AND DETECTION

Would individuals give up a token of their privacy to defend their digital identity more appropriately against mounting threats? Every person should have a right to privacy, to the extent that this right does not conflict with the law of the land. How far would each institution go to secure the identity and privacy of their customers most effectively? Would institutions go beyond issuing a privacy proclamation supported by internal policies and aligned with regulatory mandates?

Financial institutions typically secure their digital assets in the utmost robust manner that is possible. They should build on the intrinsic trust of their relationship with each customer and adopt a sincere and transparent role as defense champions of identity and privacy rights.

Reputable providers of digital services should do the same. Breaking any knee-jerk isolation posture, a possible first step would be to champion the effective protection of customer identities and privacy. *Exhibit 26* depicts such protection, as well as other concurrent actions that build up a significantly strong defense.

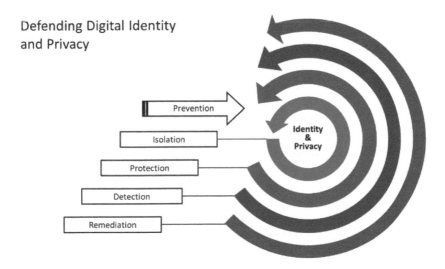

Exhibit 26 – Defending digital identity and privacy

In a digitally interconnected world, it would be naïve to expect that such defenses would never be breached. Therefore, financial institutions must adopt a security posture that supplements protective measures with intelligent and immediate detection capabilities that can also curtail and remediate any intrusion on the spot before it can compromise vital resources and spread out. Furthermore, they should invest in preventative actions, such as providing customers and employees with constant education and guidance on privacy, identity, and digital security matters.

DIGITAL PROTECTION

Facing continual mutations of increasingly sophisticated digital attacks, the threats to personal identity and privacy will become more pervasive and daunting. What protective actions should financial institutions take to safeguard the personal information that their clients, customers and members have entrusted to them?

For starters, an early detection of looming attacks will allow institutions to strengthen their defenses. Large volumes of financial transaction data, together with suspicious activity and attempted cyberattacks, which institutions around the world operate in real-time, represents a powerful source of collective intelligence. How can any one institution tap the warnings of such global source?

The answer requires thinking out-of-the-box a little. Other industries, as well as government agencies, have a line of sight to far larger volumes of digital transaction data than that of financial institutions. And most importantly, the cloud processing centers of dominant providers of digital services such as Amazon, Facebook, Google, and Microsoft will be handling most of the transaction traffic. Which means that the global source of intelligence will come from the cloud.

Even the largest financial institution lacks access to monitor all the transactions that flow globally in real time. Furthermore, navigating such vast quantities of data should require such a mighty computing power that would escape the financial and technology capacity of any institution. Fortunately, large cloud providers already have such digital security and intelligence capabilities in place and are continually improving their abilities to fend off cyberattacks and protect personal information.

As all personal information becomes digital, financial institutions should realize how ineffective it is to protect their data through sheer isolation. Sound detection and protection strategies call for thoughtful partnerships with cloud providers that have and maintain best in class digital defenses. What identity and privacy benefits would financial institutions gain from such strategic partnerships?

A MATTER OF LEADERSHIP

Several jurisdictions, both in the US and internationally, have strict regulatory compliance mandates for data residency, especially for personally identifiable information. Most predictably, strict rules constraining the movement of personal data abroad or outside local jurisdictions has triggered knee-jerk reactions in many financial institutions.

The immediate mantra has been to keep all computer processing in-house. In such a predicament, institutions would forgo the benefits of a public cloud, which could process and store personal data globally at unspecified locations. In the case of private banking or restricted accounts, the prospect of data moving abroad and personal information at risk of being compromised might lead to public scandal.

That is a perfect excuse for the traditional technology mindset of many financial institutions of processing everything on the premises, which becomes ingrained in the corporate culture, like a stubborn cyst. Technology chieftains would eschew the use of cloud computing and go to the extremes to set internal policies forbidding it. In the digital world, would negating the omnipresence of the cloud guide a proper business and technology strategy?

That is precisely the issue! For many financial institutions, ignoring the cloud represents an imminent franchise risk. Competition is increasingly harsh, and both consumers and companies crave the advanced digital services that pop up daily from the cloud. And fintech companies are eating the lunch of many well-established financial institutions.

By looking at the resounding success of unicorns and other digital disruptors, savvy boards, CEOs, and senior lines of business executives should readily figure out the broader realities of digital services. It should not take long to realize that overly zealous technology departments may have been hanging on to their inflexible in-house computing posture and resources for too long. Here is when decisive leadership action would pay off handsomely: financial institutions must find ways to adopt the cloud.

Letting their own technology teams to do all the digital heavy lifting to modernize in-house processing into the rapidly evolving digital world would be problematic, too expensive, and would take an awfully long number of years. How then should financial institutions tap the benefits of cloud computing while preserving their regulatory and fiduciary responsibilities over personal information and privacy?

Most likely, they can achieve this by applying the same formula of orchestrating strategic partnerships for digital detection and protection with leading cloud providers. Besides securing confidential information with state-of-the-art digital assets, some leading cloud companies offer hybrid architectures.

Hybrid cloud computing has the advantage of combining the indisputable power and market leadership of the public cloud, with localized portions of private or on-premises processing that cater to any data residence mandates. In a basic scheme, for example, cloud providers may offer to localize portions of the data and processing resources within a jurisdiction that requires it.

In more advanced schemes, technology providers offer smaller cloud processors that institutions would run on the premises. Besides tapping the full benefits of the public cloud, such local cloud processors would allow institutions to triage sensitive data and keep it on the premises. These hybrid technologies will continue to advance, making the combination of public and private processing increasingly seamless.

A QUANTUM SHIELD?

Could a totally public cloud service offer the ultimate digital privacy? Surely, leading cloud providers would wield the most advanced safeguards for information security and privacy. Some financial institutions may tap commercially available protective tools. However, it would be a very tall order for institutions to develop effective security and privacy tools on their own and keep up with relentless and increasingly sophisticated malicious attacks.

Figure 16 – Cybersecurity

Securing the digital world requires unparalleled technology might and global thrust throughout a specialized ecosystem. Now, leading providers such as Google, IBM, and Microsoft have been developing a groundbreaking computing paradigm: quantum computing.

The power of quantum rises from the ability, which exists in nature, to compute diverse alternatives simultaneously. It is like exploring all the possible exit paths from a maze in just one try.

Commercial quantum computers may become available in the not-so-distant future. In any case, quantum computing already offers new ways to resolve very complex problems that would take too long to resolve with classical (linear) computers. The hearts of quantum processing engines are known as qubits, which can represent several superposed computing states, as opposed to the sequential logic of classical computers.

The dodgy race to conceive commercial physical quantum computers will go on. Meanwhile, Microsoft already touts a quantum startup offer with software tools and solutions that run on its Azure cloud (Microsoft Corporation, 2020). Such a startup development kit allows companies to begin tapping the advantages of quantum logic to tackle complex non-linear challenges and prepare for the future.

Where could quantum computing make a big difference? In science, for example, it could rapidly decode human genomes and model useful drugs or composite materials. In financial services, quantum logic might help in speeding up the computation of complex derivatives or counterparty risk. The most significant impact would redefine information security: quantum logic may break the robust encryption algorithms that financial institutions employ today to secure personal information.

The ordeal for financial institutions will be to acquire a new encryption paradigm before the attackers do. To prevail in this quest, institutions will also need to find new forms of digital personal identity.

Blockchain technology, supporting a decentralized construct, will open a viable avenue to empower individuals to own and control their digital identity. For example, Microsoft is introducing an open identity architecture based on user-generated decentralized identifiers (DIDs). These globally unique DIDs reaffirm immutability, censorship resistance, and tamper evasiveness (Microsoft Corporation, 2020). Could quantum computing add other novel safeguards for uncompromised security and privacy?

Intrinsically, quantum logic possesses a natural affinity to molecules and proteins. It would then be plausible for computing models running on an ultrafast quantum processor to rapidly encode and decode an unalterable and unique cryptographic version of human DNA.

Such digital version of DNA would serve as a most effective personal shield. This shield would be part of the ultimate protection for individual privacy. Breaking it would require a physical sample of the individual DNA, the specific quantum encryption algorithm, and access to an ultrafast quantum computer to encode or decode.

A UBIQUITOUS DIGITAL SELF

Oh, the digital world! Mary had a little lamb ... and everywhere that Mary goes, her smartphone is sure to go. It is the same with Mary's wearables that track her vitals and physical activity. Or worse, it is immaterial whether Mary would carry any digital gizmo at all: street side and in-store cameras will follow her every movement. And a growing squadron of drones will be up there tracking Mary and her surroundings.

A world where digital devices abound will bring an interesting concern to privacy: whether a person asks for it or not, their face may be readily recognizable. How come? Because the continuing advances in artificial intelligence make facial recognition use cases pervasive (e.g. authenticating a person) and difficult to regulate.

A powerful combination of face recognition and machine learning algorithms, coupled with cheap and fast cloud computing speeds, can identify a face instantly with unequivocal precision. It is all about tracking hundreds of points in the factions as they change dynamically with subtle gestures. The resulting digital facial identity is more precise than a fingerprint.

A person may not need to be physically present or exposed to snooping cameras to give away his or her identity: videoconferencing, digital video clips, or even a collection of photos shared in social media could suffice.

Videoconferencing is increasingly popular as it provides face-to-face experiences. Due to the familiar, friendly, and intuitive nature of a video chat, people may not realize that their digital faces are being inadvertently exposed.

The massive adoption of videoconferencing for stay-at-home business and personal communications during the COVID-19 pandemic may have inadvertently given away personal facial identities. Absent strict privacy controls, some irresponsible (or ill-intentioned) social media and videoconferencing providers may leak (or sell) the facial identities of unaware consumers.

Furthermore, COVID-19 gave rise to some scarily intrusive technologies. For example, contactless hand-held thermometers could sense the temperature of a person, while advanced digital sensors can also capture a broader set of vitals like the heartbeat. Intelligent cameras can estimate the age and mood of a person. Whether installed on the ceiling or mounted on a drone, such cameras could tell whether physical proximity between individuals would observe the 6-foot minimum of social distancing.

Contact tracing is another feature introduced along with the testing and early warning mechanisms of COVID-19. Thanks to this feature, smartphones may log the recent locations where the owner has set foot, as well as the digital identity of those smartphones that came close, or the identity of a person with whom the owner established close contact.

With these tracking capabilities, health guardians may pick up a positive diagnosis and alert every person in the contact tracing list that they had been exposed to someone who had the virus infection. It is all for the public good, provided that any digital information that got captured remained anonymized.

A HUMAN RIGHT TO DIGITAL PROTECTION

Riding on the advances of quantum computing, blockchain, and other powerful technologies, could financial institutions, cloud services providers, or government agencies guarantee a totally secure privacy paradigm? Notwithstanding their increasingly advanced capabilities, a better question would be whether individuals and businesses could absolutely entrust them with private information. Most people would do so, however, individuals may still want to control their information on their own.

Quantum computing will eventually break classical encryption and beget a new information security paradigm. Then, equipping individuals with enterprise-grade quantum security could provide powerful protection.

But quantum security might also morph into a damaging weapon for cyberattacks. There are many other digital tools that operate with different grades of sophistication to serve distinctive military, commercial, and personal purposes, such as satellite digital imaging with varying degrees of resolution and night vision goggles.

By the same token, institutions would end up offering high-grade quantum security while individuals may still have control of a low-grade version. A combined hybrid of such improved personal protection and high-grade enterprise security would provide a trusted solution for the most demanding individuals.

Of course, institutions will offer much more than digital

protection. Like the ethical walls that separate access to banking from investment services, institutions will continue to build up the digital barriers between personal information that they maintain for different products and service purposes. And they will offer better choices and tools to keep a digital distance between themselves, the institution, and other parties that they happen to involve in the financial transactions.

The continuing evolution of digital defenses and threats will require a principled and proactive approach. Institutional ethics, as well as laws and regulations will play a key role as will preventative techniques, education to the public, and pervasive alertness to detect new threats.

Creative attackers will keep trying to steal the authenticated digital passes and authorization processes that grant access to personal information. And they will use stolen credentials to impersonate someone in the digital world and concoct a credible social media and videoconferencing presence. Or perhaps, blending the physical with the virtual digital worlds, they will impersonate villain avatars using fake identities.

REFERENCES

Britannica, E. (1995). *The New Encyclopaedia Britannica, Macro-pedia, vol 8, pp 738.* Encyclopaedia Britannica, Inc.

Lennon-McCartney (1968). Revolution 9 [Recorded by T. Beatles].

Microsoft Corporation. (2020). *Azure Quantum.* Retrieved from Microsoft Azure: https://azure.microsoft.com/en-us/services/quantum/

Microsoft Corporation. (2020). *Own your digital identity.* Retrieved from Security: https://www.microsoft.com/en-us/security/business/identity/own-your-identity

Smith, B. a. (2019). *Tools and Weapons.* Penguin Publishing Group - ISBN 9781984877727.

State of California Department of Justice. (2018). *California Consumer Privacy Act (CCPA).* Retrieved from Office of the Attorney General: https://www.oag.ca.gov/privacy/ccpa

US Federal Trade Commission. (2019). *FTC Consumer Sentinel Network.* Retrieved from Federal Trade Commission: https://public.tableau.com/profile/federal.trade.commission#!/vizhome/TheBigViewAllSentinelReports/CategoriesRanked

Wikipedia. (n.d.). *Consolidated Appropriations Act, 2018.* Retrieved from Wikipedia: https://en.wikipedia.org/wiki/Consolidated_Appropriations_Act,_2018

ABOUT THE AUTHORS

MARK SIEVEWRIGHT has won recognition as a trusted advisor to America's credit unions and is a renowned financial services industry thought leader and consultant. With more than thirty-five years of experience gained in senior leadership positions at HSBC, MasterCard International, Payment Systems Inc., TowerGroup and Fiserv, Mark has presented at hundreds of industry conferences and events, delivering informative and engaging keynote sessions focused on industry trends and, in particular, the evolution of technology and its impact. Mark established his own advisory firm in 2017 and works closely with credit unions and technology firms on business and technology strategy. In 2010 he was merited the prestigious Ambassador Award by the World Council of Credit Unions. Mark is a native of Wales, UK, and became a US citizen in 2012.

    GUILLERMO KOPP drives complex digital transformation programs at Microsoft, and his career spans over thirty years in the financial services industry. Before joining Microsoft, Guillermo served as the executive director of TowerGroup (now Gartner), and sixteen years as international staff at Citigroup, across consumer, corporate, and private banking lines of business, and also at boards of subsidiaries. Sought for his insights and strategic vision, he has presented at numerous industry events and been featured in broadcast media. Earlier in his career, Guillermo served as the corporate CIO of Aerolineas Argentinas, and also in the International Air Transport Association in Switzerland. He earned a master of science in project management from George Washington University and a computer science degree from the University of Buenos Aires. He is a native of Argentina and became a US citizen in 2003.

INDEX